A LIFE AT THE CHALK FACE

A Life at the Chalk Face

by

ROGER GRIFFITHS

The Memoir Club

© Roger Griffiths 2002

First published in 2002 by
The Memoir Club
Whitworth Hall
Spennymoor
County Durham

British Library Cataloguing in
Publication Data.
A catalogue record for this book
is available from the
British Library.

ISBN: 1 84104 036 3

Typeset by George Wishart & Associates, Whitley Bay.
Printed by Bookcraft (Bath) Ltd.

To my wife and three daughters

Contents

Illustrations ix

Foreword xi

Introduction xiii

Chapter 1 1

Chapter 2 8

Chapter 3 18

Chapter 4 41

Chapter 5 52

Chapter 6 67

Chapter 7 83

Chapter 8 95

Chapter 9 105

Chapter 10 117

Chapter 11 133

Chapter 12 149

Chapter 13 168

Chapter 14 190

Chapter 15 199

Index 207

Bibliography 210

Illustrations

The author (1964) on appointment to Hurstpierpoint xiv

The author with parents and brother, Richard,
(November 1939) 3

The author with Granny Griffiths and brother, Richard,
in the garden of 'Green Meadow' (1938) 4

Llandrindod (1940) 11

Lancing (1949) 23

Teme House, Summer 1948 25

Lancing Chapel from the cricket field 31

1957 – A successful year of bowls 50

A rehearsal of Henry IV part I at Charterhouse 79

April 2nd 1966 114

HMS Pinafore: Captain, author; Dick Deadeye,
Christopher Dean 120

Oliver: Mr Bumble, Neil Page; Mr Brownlow, author 121

The Chapel Hurstpierpoint College 124

The Hurst Common Room 1973 129

The School and House Prefects 1970 141

The School Prefects and Bumble (12 weeks old) 1980 142

The family about 1974 158

The opening of the Frank Mason Science Laboratories,
May 1985 166

A reluctant commuter returns home, 1987 172

Dinner at the Mansion House, 1991 180

The family grows, 1993 185

Off to the Palace – Garden Party, 1991 189

My parents (about 1976) 203

Foreword

John Moore

(sometime Headmaster of The King's School, Worcester)

WHEN I WAS ASKED by Roger to write this Foreword, I had no idea what I would be attempting to introduce. Yes, I knew that he had been working on his memoirs – memoirs which I may say some of his friends had been somewhat apprehensive about because of his wicked sense of humour and elephantine memory – but what would be the result? Still, just as all good prefaces are written last, so this is written after reading the proofs – and it is a real pleasure and honour to be able to add a few words.

Sadly, I only got to know Roger and Diana when I joined that splendid 'club', the Headmasters' Conference. It might have been otherwise, for I was interviewed by Brian Young when Roger was teaching at Charterhouse, but it transpired that I was one of those he summoned, as he put it, 'to see what was on the market'. There was no job; I wish there had been.

After his origins and early childhood in his beloved Wales, Roger takes us through formative years at Lancing, in Cambridge, Oxford and Paris, to teaching Modern Languages and a Headship at an early age. Then, after a long and distinguished 'reign' at Hurstpierpoint, he was invited to move to HMC to look after members' interests. This was an inspired appointment by those leading HMC at the time, and put Roger in a post which he totally transformed to the enormous benefit of the Conference. Three incarnations for Roger: as an inspiring teacher, as a caring Headmaster and as father-confessor and friend to over two hundred HMC colleagues.

The world of education these days is beset by constant change, and in danger of becoming appallingly utilitarian, not least through Government diktat. Here we have a picture of a time when central to study at school and university, and at the heart of teaching thereafter, were learning, and what Walter Oakeshott described as a conversation between the generations in which the young are initiated into those aspects of our culture which are worth preserving. Throughout, there are delightful vignettes, and pictures of an age which is probably gone for ever. How many can now teach as Roger did? How many Headmasters now have – or should I say make – the time to teach a sizeable timetable and to produce plays?

Despite his claim that these are 'meandering memoirs', throughout there are underlying threads: a passionate care for his charges and a devotion to scholarship, a deep-seated faith founded and nurtured in the Woodard tradition, a lifelong passion for music and an ever-present sense of the absurd. And supporting all this are Diana and his daughters who are the bedrock of his happiness.

I hope that many – whether they know Roger or not – will enjoy this picture of a life devoted to the young and to their success. Yes indeed, it has been *A Life at the Chalk Face*, and not just before he moved to work for HMC, for even then Roger's many and sometimes difficult duties, for instance guiding wayward colleagues or confronting misguided Boards of Governors, were all ultimately designed to ensure that education should be at its best for each individual pupil wherever he touched their lives. There are few higher callings.

Introduction

IN THE COURSE OF writing these memoirs two things have struck me very forcibly. The first is how very lucky I have been throughout my life. I was born into a very happy and united family. Apart from prep. school days my own schooling – in pre-war Barry and post-war Lancing – were most enjoyable. Cambridge, and then Oxford, was a wonderful experience, student teaching at Westminster, and then as an 'assistant' in Paris provided unlimited opportunities for getting to know those two great cities and the musical, theatrical and cultural life associated with them.

Then Charterhouse, a great school, and a place where I made friends who have remained that throughout my life. A year in America was a great experience and here too life-long friends were made, people whom I may not see for five or ten years but with whom we begin where we left off – the time lapse is immaterial. Hurstpierpoint gave me the happiest years of all, not least because of the joy of marriage and a family who are a devoted group. Then working for and with 240 Headmasters in HMC for eleven years with a warm welcome wherever I went in the country. And finally, retirement, with new friendships in Chichester, Cocking and Petworth House – I have indeed been a fortunate man and do not regret any part of my seventy years existence.

The other striking thought is how very fortunate I have been in my choice of wife. A wonderful and loving mother, caring wife, the perfect model of a Headmaster's wife, a good secretary and P.A. and help with all problems – and she has even typed up the whole of this manuscript despite my appalling handwriting!

This 'life at the chalk face' has indeed been a happy and blessed one for which I am eternally grateful.

The author (1964) on appointment to Hurstpierpoint.

Chapter 1

At Flores in the Azores where Sir Richard Grenville lay,
And a pinnace, like a fluttered bird, came flying from far away:
'Spanish ships of war at sea! We have sighted fifty three!'

> Lars Porsena of Clusium
> By the nine gods he swore
> That the great house of Tarquin
> Should suffer wrong no more.
> By the Nine Gods he swore it,
> And named a trysting day
> And bade his messengers ride forth,
> East and West and South and North,
> To summon his array.

THOSE AND SOME SIX OR SEVEN of the other great classic poems of English literature remain one of my earliest memories. Our housekeeper/cook/nanny, Beatrice, a simple soul born on a farm in the Vale of Glamorgan, and the mainstay of our family for the first few years of my life, had learnt them at her school and would recite them to my brother and myself as she put us to bed. She was a remarkable person and a very great help to my dear mother as she made a family home for us.

We lived in a detached brown-shingled house, Green Meadow at Romilly Park, Barry, Glamorganshire. My father was a solicitor in the town – to whom many of the older residents went because he was bilingual – Welsh and English – and they preferred to conduct their business in Welsh. My father had only spoken Welsh until the age of seven and another early memory I have is when visiting his mother, my Granny. If they did not wish the children to hear what they were discussing, they spoke in Welsh. At a later date, my brother and I thought we might learn the language to break this habit, but although we were both Modern Linguists, we were defeated by the intricacies of the Welsh language. My father always listened to the Welsh News on the radio and as I grew older, it was possible to get the gist of the story being reported, as since the sixteenth century English words have been adapted into the language, e.g. *telewele* for television. Some years later, after the War, when French onion sellers from Brittany would bring their wares to the house, my brother and I could converse with them in French, my father not understanding, and my father could speak with them in Welsh – to our discomfort!

Life in the thirties was very peaceful. The house we lived in had been designed by my mother. She was the youngest of three sisters and could have become a professional singer, but from her earliest years had suffered from an almost pathological nervousness of travelling around or doing anything in public. She had also trained as a pharmacist but never put it into practice. Her parents lived in Barry.

Grandpa Hill had been an engineer at sea but on retirement had undertaken management of the Barry Dock Hotel, where the girls had been brought up. Just before the War, they retired to a village near Barry where Grandpa cultivated a fruit orchard and they lived peacefully. A great treat was to visit them and play (or sleep) in a genuine gipsy caravan which was parked beside their house.

My father's parents also lived in Barry in a large house overlooking the bay which led to Barry Island, the South Wales pleasure resort. Grandpa Griffiths had been a very successful grocer in the Welsh valley town of Porth. He had married one of the daughters of 'the big house'. My great grandfather, William Mathias, had been a colliery landowner and lived at Tynycymmer Hall with his large family of nine children, of whom my grandmother was the third, born in 1869. She was only 4 ft 10 inches high but ruled her husband and one son (my father) with a rod of iron. There were five daughters, all of whom were strict teetotallers. On my great

The author with parents and brother, Richard, (November 1939).

grandfather's death, the family were all left a considerable amount of money which enabled my grandfather to retire (to Barry) where he became a J.P. and pillar of the local Bowling Club. My great uncle, Richard, decided – at the age of 25 – to retire and devote himself to hunting, shooting and fishing. To his sisters' horror he drank two bottles of whisky a day. At the age of 75 his doctor told him to cut it down, so he took to one bottle a day and died – a happy bachelor – at the age of 84. I never met him but I remember my brother working out that a vessel of 1,000 tons could have been floated on the amount of neat whisky he had consumed in his lifetime!

My parents played tennis and golf but led a quiet life. My greatest excitement was to be allowed – occasionally – to ride around Romilly Park with Mr Cruise the milkman on the back of his milkfloat when he was delivering to all the houses. His old horse moved slowly but it was a great thrill for a small boy.

Very often on a Sunday afternoon we would go out in the car, a Rover 14, BTX 425, for a drive around the Vale of Glamorgan, and every six months or so we would call in at Lake Farm, Cowbridge.

*The author with Granny Griffiths and brother, Richard, in the garden of
'Green Meadow' (1938).*

This was one of five small farms which my father had inherited
from his great grandfather (incidentally, the only one still in our
possession today). There, the old lady of the house would entertain
us to tea and Welsh cakes in the kitchen where sides of bacon hung
from the ceiling. Inevitably the visit ended with a substantial piece
of one of these, together with eggs and farm butter being packed
into the car – a very welcome addition to our diet at home.

That car lasted a long time. On one occasion my father returned
late one evening from a day's shooting in the valleys, bearing with
him several large pieces of lamb! He had not shot a lamb but in the
dark driving back over the Brecon Beacons had, unfortunately,
killed a lamb. One of his companions in the car was a local butcher
and he had disposed of the carcase between the four of them – not a
very respectable story to narrate about an eminently respectable
local solicitor I fear!

The great excitement of Summer 1935 was the arrival on the scene of my younger brother Richard. We have always had a very close relationship and right from the first it was good to have a companion. His birthday is June 21st and for me that proved a blessing. My own birthday is December 25th (hence my second name, Noel) and from an early age it was clear that that date has decided disadvantages for those born on it. One present does for both birthday and Christmas. Also there was even a marked shortage of birthday cards for Christmas cards to the whole family would arrive with 'and a happy birthday to Roger' being written at the foot of them. My mother resolved the situation by saying that we would exchange Christmas presents at Christmas and birthday presents on June 21st and she continued that custom until her death just before her 95th birthday! Nevertheless, Christmas Day was always Christmas Day and has only really been celebrated as a birthday since my marriage in 1966. My dear wife, Diana, insists that we have a light birthday lunch (often smoked salmon and champagne) and tea with birthday cake, and Christmas is celebrated with dinner – for the last few years and to everyone's satisfaction with goose rather than turkey, followed by Christmas pudding and mince pies. But I retain every sympathy with all those whose birthdays occur very near to Christmas Day.

All four grandparents would visit us regularly – one such visit resulted in a disaster for my brother and myself! We thought that we would put on an entertainment for them all – I had a toy trumpet and Richard (aged 3) had a drum. My father was a lapsed Freemason and we had found in a drawer his regalia, including an apron and medals. Clad in these we threw open the drawing room door and marched in. One grandfather, a non-Mason, was much amused; the other grandfather, an enthusiastic Mason, was furious. We were hustled from the room, given a wallop with my father's leather razor strop and sent to bed without supper. The incident was never mentioned again.

Each August was the family holiday – always to the same place,

Llandrindod Wells in mid-Wales. This small provincial town had seen its heyday towards the end of the nineteenth century when it became the leading spa of mid-Wales. There were a remarkable number of very large, luxurious hotels built and a railway line, the Central Wales line from Swansea to Shrewsbury, brought many visitors to the town. It also had the largest number of public conveniences ever seen in a small town. The reason – the course of waters to be taken at the Pump House in the Rock Park Gardens (three different varieties which to the uninitiated were known as salt water, ink and sulphur) consisted of one glass before breakfast, one late afternoon the first day, two glasses the second day, three the third and up to six on the sixth day and then decreasing – five the seventh day to one the eleventh day – and if your hotel was any distance from the Pump Room the conveniences were an essential part of life.

But we did not go to take the waters – at least my grandfather did occasionally – we were there for the Annual Lawn Bowls Tournament, the largest in Wales, which lasted over three weeks and which drew competitors from all over the United Kingdom. My father was runner-up in the major singles trophy in 1933 and won the Open Pairs Championship of Wales in 1935, so we had cause for celebration. It was good to meet up with the same people each year and the little town with its Victorian atmosphere in the buildings had its own attraction. There will be more of this later in my story.

In Barry, life went on its own peaceful way – the annual flower and agricultural show every July in Romilly Park, the big event of the year. Both my parents played golf, my mother tennis and my father bowls and my brother and I were spoilt by our grandparents. We had a succession of dogs – bulldog Jem followed by bull mastiff Leo and then a spaniel Laddie. It is good for children to grow up with an animal in the household and ours were all pets of the greatest importance.

One event from that time still stands out in my memory. Granny

Griffiths had decided that I was to have a special treat. She took me to the local cinema in Barry to a performance of Walt Disney's *Snow White and the Seven Dwarfs*. What she did not know, and what I have come to realize since, is that there is always some scene or scenes of violence or terror in those wonderful Disney cartoons. I was terrified, not so much of the wicked Queen, though she was quite an horrific character, but of the old woman into whom she transformed herself to give Snow White the polished apple. The result was nightmares at home for some months to follow. I tried to bear this in mind as our three daughters were growing up later.

And so we reached 1939 – but to a 7 and a $3^1/2$ year old pair of brothers there was no sense or meaning in grown-ups' talk of War. The first changes in September were the arrival in Romilly Park of a barrage balloon unit, the digging up of much of the park into allotments for growing vegetables and the conversion of the downstairs back room into an air raid shelter with bunk beds for Richard and myself. Barry was at that time quite an important port and soon we began to hear the ghastly sound of air raid alarms which meant getting up and going downstairs to the bunk beds. The only major incident to affect us was a great crash of broken glass one night – the barrage balloon had broken loose from its mooring and the cable had gone through our landing window! But we were soon sleeping downstairs every night.

And then came the first real change. My father joined the RAF Volunteer Reserve and was posted to Essex. We missed him greatly and saw him very infrequently. Then in the summer of 1940 my mother heard that he was to go abroad. We all (my mother, Richard and I) went by train to Braintree in Essex where we stayed in a village pub with, for us boys, the excitement of a pianola with some piano rolls in our bedroom. This kept us amused for hours but after three days it was goodbye to father and we returned to Barry with a tearful mother. Thank goodness Beatrice was there to pick up the pieces. I was now eight years old – the man of the family – but not really of much use I fear.

Chapter 2

THE RAIDS CONTINUED on a near nightly basis – and by September 1940 my mother took the great decision that we should leave Barry and evacuate – and Llandrindod seemed the obvious choice. To us boys it was a great excitement. Looking back on it I am amazed that my dear mother, that quiet and gentle soul, could have embarked into the unknown as she did but nevertheless that is what happened. We did, of course, know a few of the residents there – and so together with Beatrice the ever dependable, we set off from Barry. Train to Cardiff, change; second train to Bargoed, change; third train to Three Cocks Junction, change; fourth train to Builth Wells and then taxi for the last seven miles to Llandrindod. The whole journey was 80 miles and took the best part of a day!

On arrival we went to the Beaufort Hotel which we had known from bowling visits. Miss Whatmough, the proprietress, made us very welcome and set about helping my mother find somewhere pleasant to live. Within a few days, we moved to Glen View, Park Terrace, a small modern house overlooking the Rock Park, owned by Mrs Richards, a motherly Welsh lady who welcomed us into her family. She had three daughters and a son – two of the daughters were married and the son was in the Army – so there was plenty of room for us in the house. Another evacuee family was there also, a Mrs Tibbenham with her son John who had come from Croydon.

Mrs Tibby, as she became swiftly known to us boys, was a forceful personality and she and our mother hit it off immediately and became very good friends. The two families were to remain together throughout the rest of the War. The next thing to resolve

was school. I had been sent at the age of 4½ to St Baruc's School –
a ten minute walk from our house. The Headmistress, Mrs Jones,
seemed to me at the time a formidable personage – which is very
right and proper – but I met her many years later and found that
she was a kind and caring person, not nearly as old as I had
imagined!

We were extremely well taught. In arithmetic we learnt not only
our tables up to twelve times but also thirteen, seventeen and
nineteen times tables, and it is quite remarkable how useful these
have been throughout my life. We also began French at the age of
seven and that has been the foundation of my life thereafter. There
was a large garden at the school where we could play, but even at
that early age it became very clear that I was not to be a sportsman
in any way whatsoever. In this respect I must have been the
greatest disappointment to my father for he had excelled at all
sports. He had been in the Shrewsbury School Cricket XI for four
years, in the Hockey XI for three years, later playing both games at
County level as an amateur. He had been cox in the Shrewsbury
VIII – he was only 5 foot 7 inches tall and weighed only 7 stone 9
pounds (which he remained until his latter years), and played fives,
and ran cross country for the School. Later in life he played golf
with a handicap of 2 and then bowls at County level. He was, in
fact, Secretary of the Welsh Bowling Association and the first
President of the International Bowling Board. I shall speak more of
this later.

In Llandrindod Wells a small girls' school, Micklesfield, had
come up from the South Coast and was established in a church
hall in the town and so we went there as they were taking boys up
to the age of 9, to increase numbers no doubt. It was an atmosphere not too dissimilar from St Baruc's and so we continued to
learn well. I suppose I am one of the few members of HMC to be
a former pupil of a GSA school!

But it was soon my ninth birthday and it was decided that I
should go to the Llandrindod Wells Grammar School; a very

different affair. I shall never forget my first day there. I was put in the first form and together with 31 other boys awaited the arrival of our form master (whom I shall call Mr Thomas). On the stroke of nine a large man appeared and we all stood – in silence – as he unlocked a cupboard and laid out on his desk a piece of wood with a handle and six canes of varying thicknesses, ending with the most whippy. He then told us to sit down and announced 'spelling'. We went around the class, one by one. If a mistake was made, the boy in question was summoned out, told to bend over the desk and given one stroke of the piece of wood on the backside. If the same boy made a second mistake, it was the same procedure but cane no. 1 (the thickest) was used and so on it went for half an hour. Then came the announcement 'mental arithmetic' and a similar procedure took place. After another half hour, it was break time and thereafter lessons were on the usual variety of subjects – all taught by Mr Thomas. The shock to the system of a timid soul used to the gentle ways of St Baruc's and Micklesfield was considerable but I had been well taught at both those establishments and so survived the daily first hour for several weeks without any punishment. My fellow pupils were mostly farmer's sons and totally unfazed by anything.

Then one morning I progressed to cane no. 2 on mental arithmetic. It didn't really hurt and I thought nothing of it until I related it on my return to Glen View to an aghast audience of my mother, Beatrice and brother Richard. The result was, for me, catastrophic. My mother set off for the school with a reluctant son in tow, marched in and demanded to see the Headmaster. He politely but firmly refused to discipline Mr Thomas, whereupon my mother stated that she was withdrawing me from the school and we exited, to my acute embarrassment, and as was to prove very soon, to my great disadvantage.

The interesting thing is that some twenty years later while holidaying in Llandrindod, I revisited the school and found that Mr Thomas was still teaching there and still using the same

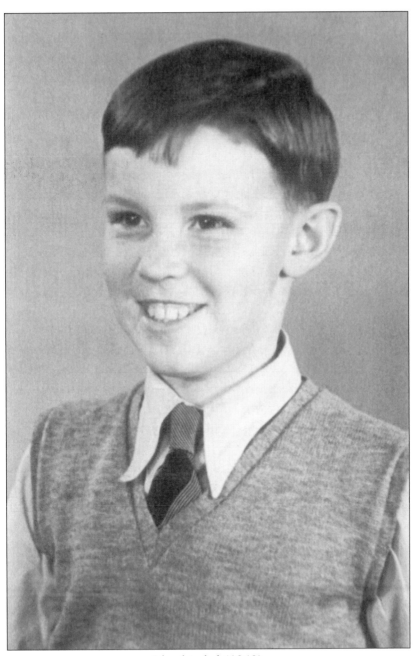

Llandrindod (1940).

methods! Of course, nowadays in 2001 such methods would be front page news in the tabloid press and Mr Thomas would not be a member of the teaching profession – indeed would be fortunate not to be in prison, so litigious have parents become. Nevertheless, I must admit that there was considerable merit behind it all for good spelling and alert mental arithmetic are a great asset to anyone in whatever profession or walk of life.

But there was now the great problem of my education! On making enquiries around, my mother learnt that a preparatory school (from Rednal, Birmingham as it happens) had evacuated to Brampton Bryan Hall, a large country house some 20 miles from Llandrindod. She and Mrs Tibby paid a visit and came back to tell me that they had found a 'lovely new school for me'. And so I went to the Lickey Hills School, Headmaster Harry Healey, a tall, hard Old Wykehamist. Brampton Bryan Hall was in a lovely situation – a rambling old country house with ornate gardens and a ruined castle in its grounds. The staff were elderly but on the whole good schoolmasters and schoolmistresses and my first term passed by quite pleasantly with several visits from my mother and Mrs Tibby. The Headmaster, was, however, a games fanatic who despised anyone who was incapable of or did not want to participate in games, which boded ill for a happy future for me.

Latin was taught by Mr Harry, a delightful old scholar, the typical prep school master, who devoted his life to ensuring that the boys in his charge enjoyed the subject and enjoyed life at school. Mr Kidd taught Geography and was a strict disciplinarian; Miss Peters, young and charming, taught French, at which I got on well thanks to my early St Baruc's training, and the Headmaster taught mathematics with iron discipline. His son and daughter were both pupils in the school, she the only girl with some 70 boys and I think he was harder on them even than on any other pupils. Towards the end of my first term, the bombshell announcement was made that he had decided to move the school back to Rednal, 'where we could be under proper school conditions and discipline'.

My heart sank at the thought of being much further away from my family.

And so in Summer 1941 we made the train journey from Llandrindod to Birmingham via Shrewsbury. From the centre of Birmingham there was a twelve mile tram journey to Rednal and then a two mile walk to the school which was set up on the Lickey Hills. As we trudged up the drive, the buildings looked sombre – and sombre indeed was the next term for me.

I have always felt considerable sympathy for those pupils who have no athletic ability whatsoever. This is partly because I am one of those myself. Harry Healey did not feel that way. I was a marked man because I did not throw myself wholeheartedly into games. In the gym, it was worse. He would stand with a leather strap in hand and beat me or any other unfortunate until I or he managed to claw the way up a climbing rope and would then look on with amusement as I slid down too fast and burnt my hands on the rope. On the football field (leased to a local farmer and semi-cleared of cow dung before each game by the pupils) he would ensure that those of us who had no ability at – and indeed no interest in – the game were held up to ridicule and discomfort. It was no wonder that when I went back for the start of my third term I did not hand in my term's pocket money!

On the third day of term after breakfast, my school cap firmly in my pocket, I sneaked out of the school, down the long drive and two miles to the tram depot in Rednal. Then 12 miles into Birmingham, constantly looking out of the back window of the tram in case Harry Healey's car was tearing down the road after me. Then to the railway station and a train to Shrewsbury. A two hour wait on Shrewsbury station platform, all the time imagining that I could see the terrifying figure of Harry Healey coming along the platform with cane in hand. (He would beat pupils on the arm as it drew blood more easily!) Then the slow Central Wales line train to Llandrindod Wells arriving there late in the afternoon. I made my way to where we were now living – in a house in Ithon

Road – and was welcomed with tearful astonishment. My mother rang the school at once – the Headmaster said that he had assumed I was in the San. – the San Sister of course had no knowledge of me. From what I know now of schools, it reveals a total lack of supervision of pupils, but nevertheless I was taken back to school the next day and left in floods of tears.

The Headmaster never forgave me. The one asset from the whole experience was that on the (fortunately very rare) occasions that a boy ran away from Hurstpierpoint College when I was Headmaster there, I could say to him on his return – 'I know what pressure you must have been under because I ran away from my school when I was a pupil there. But I know now, which I did not know then, and which you do not know now, how much worry and heartache you cause to your family and the people here who love you. I would like to have you here still as a pupil – please come back, but it is on one condition – you must promise me that if you ever get to feeling that you are going to do it again because you cannot stand it here, you will not run away but will come here to talk to me or to my wife or my secretary or your Housemaster, so that one of us can help.'

But that was not my fate. The Headmaster managed to make my remaining years in his school as unpleasant as he could without actually driving me to run away again. But not all life was unpleasant. The masters and mistresses were generally friendly and encouraging. At the age of eleven I had the choice of German or Geography, German taught by Miss Peters and Geography by Mr Kidd. There was no real choice and so I became and remain a Modern Linguist. My younger brother Richard joined me at the Lickey Hills School. He is an exceptionally intelligent person and was even then and so as the elder brother I could forget my own miseries whilst trying to look after him and protect him from those who were jealous of his academic ability. We even won the school doubles tennis trophy – quite a success for me as a real non-starter athlete.

At the age of 12 I had appendicitis and was rushed to Bromsgrove Cottage Hospital. My mother came up with a friend from Llandrindod who was also the local ambulance driver and I was driven back in state to recuperate at home.

Time was now moving on and my mother was asked by the Headmaster to which school I was to proceed. My father, my uncles and my cousins had all been to Shrewsbury and it had always been assumed that Richard and I would go there. However, my dear father had gone off to the War in 1939 having failed to enter me for the school and the reply to Lickey Hills was that their lists were full. My mother consulted Harry Healey. Lancing College had been evacuated to the Ludlow area for the duration of the War and, as at Brampton Bryan, there had been contacts with them. And so it was decided that I should go to Lancing. Harry Healey, anti RNPG to the end, would not allow me to sit for the Scholarship Examination (I passed out top of the Common Entrance list of 100 pupils as it happened) and his final report on me to my prospective Housemaster read: 'I can see no future for him. He will come to no good.' I learnt later in life that my housemaster at Lancing wrote a card to Harry Healey when I passed my School Certificate and another at Higher Certificate one year later, again when I went to King's College Cambridge, again when I became Sixth Form French Master at Charterhouse and a final card when I was appointed Headmaster at Hurstpierpoint College at the age of 32 – the last apparently with a note appended saying: 'I should not think of trying to enter any of your boys there if I were you!' In fact, out of sympathy for them I am sure I would have made every effort to accept them!

Meanwhile life in Llandrindod went on amiably. Each year there was a splendid pantomime in the theatre, The Albert Hall, and there was tea music each afternoon by a resident trio in the Pump Room in the Rock Park Gardens. My mother and Mrs Tibby worked in the local NAAFI stores and we got to know some of the officer cadets from the OCTU stationed in the town.

This meant invitations to the cadets' passing out parades, with pomp and splendour – I have always loved and still do love a military band. For years my family and I have been regular attenders at the Royal Tournament at Earls Court. How sad that that spectacular event is no more. At Llandrindod, the big hotels were gradually closing to become government and county offices of various departments. But there were still three magnificent putting courses and the lake for boating and – if you were feeling really adventurous – a ride up to the Golf Links and back from the Automobile Palace in a magnificent 1920s bus 'Colonel Bogey' – 9d up and 6d down – the journey was perilous in the extreme.

Of war, apart from the activities of the OCTU, there was very little sign. Admittedly rationing, and particularly sweet rationing, was ever present in our minds but we still managed to eat well. Twice a year we would make the journey down to Barry (still all the changes of train) to visit my grandparents. Grandpa Griffiths had died in 1940 and Granny Griffiths lived on in her large house by the sea; Granny and Grandpa Hill always had a supply of apples and plums to give us.

There was one air raid a year at Llandrindod – or so it seemed to us. It was usually a German bomber which had got lost after bombing the Midlands and no damage was sustained in our immediate area but it provided a little excitement for the resident population.

Just before I sat the Common Entrance Examination came a real excitement. My father had spent three years of the War in Egypt in the RAF as a Codes and Ciphers Officer. He was then in Italy and finally was in the first plane to land in Norway where German troops who had surrendered were still much in evidence. Now suddenly he arrived in Llandrindod. For me, having spent the last $5^{1}/_{2}$ years as the 'man of the family' it came as a shock. This man, whom I really did not know, not having seen him since 1940 was back in our family life and I was being told what to do. My mother had brought us up to be well behaved but we had nevertheless had our own way of life and now suddenly all was changed.

Looking back on it now I can see that I must have been impossibly difficult. I resented my father being around. I am glad to say that within two to three years all had changed and I adored him as a real companion and friend until he died, sadly too young in 1979 at the age of 77. But it was he, still in RAF uniform, who took me down to Lancing by train in September 1945 to start what was to be one of the happiest periods of my life.

Chapter 3

W̶E WERE 100 NEW BOYS in a school of 300 that first September term. Lancing had come back from its evacuation in Shropshire for the Summer Term of 1945. The West Sussex Gazette published a poem which sums up the local feeling:

> But when the mayflower blossoms
> By Shropshire waters slow
> The lads who walk beside them
> Will pack their bags and go.
>
> The town will grow more silent
> And quiet be the halls
> When cottage lamps are lighted
> And misty twilight falls.
>
> The hill that stands by Shoreham
> Will wake and Sussex men
> See lights in Lancing Chapel
> And say, 'They're home agen'.

It was quite a task settling back in to Lancing. All the furniture and equipment from the various Ludlow houses had to be packed up and the houses restored to their owners in good condition; Lancing had for five years been used by the Armed Forces and so the buildings there had to be restored to their true purpose as a school. Also the whole ethos of a school had to be recovered after five years as a federation of houses. Numbers were down, and academic and sporting standards had to be re-established. And so there were a hundred of us new boys.

I was to be in Head's House, re-opening that term, House-master Sam Jagger. Sam had been South of England Squash

Champion and a Sussex County Cricketer. His first task on that first day was to take all his new boys to the squash courts to try them out. In my case the trial did not last long but among the intake were two identical twins, Peter and Michael Ball, who were to become my greatest friends. Peter was to become South of England Junior Squash Champion and a Cambridge blue; Michael was slightly less proficient at squash but very musical. He played the Mozart Piano Concerto No. 23 in A major with the school orchestra before he left.

That first evening in the Junior Dormitory, twenty beds, stone floor, no heating, we were all in bed when the Head of House, Johnny Ewer, a terrifying figure to the new boys, came in. 'This' he said 'is how you fold your clothes when in my House. Jacket, then trousers, then shirt, then pants, vest, socks and tie on top. Get out of bed and re-do yours.' We all did so and he strode around the dormitory and threw about half the piles on the floor. 'Do them again'. This time we all passed muster. 'Now there will be trouble if they are not all right tomorrow.' We were all in awe of this huge man, but I think he was a good and wise Head of House. Nineteen years later when I had just become Headmaster of Hurstpierpoint, I was invited as guest speaker to the Lancing Old Boys Club Dinner. After my speech a short, to me elderly-looking man, came up and said: 'Excuse me sir, I think we were at Lancing at the same time.' It was Johnny Ewer, but I had grown from a new boy of 5 ft 2 inches to a man of 6 ft and he was not the terrifying figure of my youth. Such is life.

There were some incredible members on the teaching staff at Lancing. Of course it was 1945 and thus many of those who had taught there throughout the War were past the age of 60 (retiring age) and near the end of their careers. It was a remarkable school particularly because of the warm and friendly atmosphere. This was in great measure due to the Headmaster, Frank Doherty. He had come to Lancing in 1935 when the school was at a low ebb. His predecessor had not been a success and numbers were down (in 1938 they stood at 232). As things began to pick up the War broke out and then evacuation in 1940 to Ludlow resulted in more problems. The school had survived the War however, and was now back in its own glorious buildings. Frank Doherty was a tired man – he had lost a lung in the First World War, despite which he smoked considerably (with a short filter), but he had the respect and liking of his staff. To see him walk around the school, there was little doubt that he was the Headmaster. He was an impressive looking man, handsome with a full head of iron-grey hair and always moved with a measured and erect authority. His face was grey also and heavily lined but he was to me as a boy in his charge a remarkable man, kind and generous hearted whom one would never seek to let down. I was in his School Certificate Divinity class. At the start of the Summer Term (eight weeks to the exams) he announced with an apology in his first lesson that we had for two terms studied the wrong texts. 'This will mean, gentlemen, a little extra effort on all our parts'. I think that I am correct in saying that we all passed the exam, though certainly in my case, by the barest margin.

His presence was felt throughout the school. For me, what he stood for and taught me and many of my contemporaries, is best summed up in two appreciations written of him when he retired in 1953. The first was by the then Provost of Lancing, Canon A.R. Browne-Wilkinson.

> There are three points in which Frank Doherty's headmastership has been outstanding. First, nothing has exercised the determination of the Headmaster more than the purpose, successfully realized, of making the religion of the school its outstanding excellence. Next in order I should put the capacity to secure the full confidence of parents. There is abounding evidence that the unremitting diligence with which parents have been given a feeling of security and certainty that their sons were in careful and caring hands has been responsible for no small part of the ever-increasing regard for the school. And thirdly should be

recorded the successful promotion of sound personal relationships all round. An outstanding characteristic of the Lancing of
today is that it is a community in which masters and boys, older
boys and younger boys, live in a spirit of friendly and trusting
happiness. This at any rate is the impression that the school has
made on one who has known it for more than fifty years.

The other appreciation was written by a remarkable master,
Basil Handford, who was appointed to Lancing in 1927 as Sixth
Form master. He spent 33 years at the school where he had been a
boy and then after two years in the USA helping to start a girls'
school in Connecticut, returned to Lancing in 1962 and continued
to teach part-time until 1979. He wrote a History of Lancing in
1930 and then an update entitled History and Memoirs published
in 1986. He wrote of his Headmaster in 1953:

> I feel that the basic reason for Frank Doherty's success as a Head
> Master has been his religious faith – 'Seek first the kingdom of
> God and all these things shall be added unto you.' This was his
> principle. His first object was to bring the school back to its prime
> purpose of giving an education based on religion. A man of
> integrity himself, he sought to make the school trustworthy and
> thereby he made it trusted. He rejected short cuts to popularity
> and made decisions in accordance with what he believed to be
> right, and thereby in the end he made it popular.
>
> He has not been the type of Head Master who sometimes earns
> the title 'great' by dominating every activity, putting a finger in
> every pie and shaping everything to a preconceived pattern,
> requiring his assistants to conform and leave all decisions to him.
> Frank Doherty dislikes the limelight, and being a very modest
> man, with a mind receptive rather than original, and remarkable
> for sound judgement, he expected and encouraged initiative in
> others and adopted their suggestions, if he found them good; and
> thus the school has grown an exuberant crop of activities. If they
> sometimes compete with each other for the light and air, they are
> at any rate instinct with a life of their own and are not a dead thing
> moulded on a potter's wheel.

He does not theorize much, or at any rate, he does not give expression to abstract theories. His judgement has always seemed to me to be intuitive and his intuition illuminated by a basic Christian attitude to life. And so he has been neither dictator nor doctrinaire but a pastor.

He went on to explain how his wise handling of the personal difficulties, not only of masters and boys, but also of domestic and maintenance staff had made Lancing a singularly happy community.

How proud I would have been had such a pronouncement been made about me when I retired from headmastering. Suffice it to say that I tried in my own way to run my school and community as Frank Doherty had run Lancing when I was there as a boy.

My first two years were uneventful. I had been placed in the Remove, the second form in the school, as a result of Common Entrance and so sat my School Certificate in Summer 1947. Head's House had been a happy experience and the Ball twins and I enjoyed ourselves, sharing everything – even the modest sweet allowance that came each day – for rationing was still in operation. During that Summer Term it had been announced that a new house was to open in September and volunteers were asked to help start it. One of the most exciting days was when Christopher Chamberlin, who had been asked to be Housemaster of the new House, invited Peter and Michael Ball and myself to help him in this task.

Christopher was one of the most remarkable schoolmasters I have ever met. He had been at Lancing as a boy and then after three years at King's College Cambridge returned to his old school where he remained until the age of 60 at which point he retired and moved to Millfield where he taught History and continued to coach athletics, primarily field sports, until he was 79. During the War he had looked after two Houses in Ludlow but on the return to Lancing had remained Housemaster of Gibbs as he had been before the War. After 15 years he was now to embark on another

Lancing (1949).

15 years but running the House in an entirely different way. He had been a very firm disciplinarian, but now beating was out. It was necessary to talk to a miscreant, to try to persuade him to admit a wrongdoing and to accept a punishment which was of benefit to the community. On the whole this worked.

Teme House, the new House, was lodged in the imposing building, which had been built for a former Headmaster to the south of the main quadrangle. The dormitories were small, the bathrooms decorated with tiles and with heated towel rails which seemed a real luxury after the coldness of Head's House. The choice of volunteers to start the House had been most skilfully done. Three were taken from each year group in the school, apart from the lowest form, to ensure that for the first four years of the new House there would be senior members of the House with some experience of the school. There were with these twelve, fourteen new boys that first term, September 1947. When Head's House had re-opened in September 1945 the 'volunteers' drafted in from other Houses were only from the top three forms so that, with 20 new boys the first term, one of them would be Head of House in three years' time. As it happened, that worked quite well as there were one or two more mature characters among the twenty.

Teme House, named after the river in Shropshire which had flowed near the country houses occupied by the school, flourished and Christopher Chamberlin certainly knew his boys and cared for them. I was still receiving a birthday letter with news particularly of my contemporaries in the House up until the year that he died. He once told me that from the thirty years he had as a Housemaster, nearly fifty percent of his boys either went into the church or into teaching. My own particular friends Peter and Michael founded their own monastic order, the Community of the Glorious Ascension, within the Church of England, and they ended up Peter as Bishop of Gloucester and Michael as Bishop of Truro. It is certainly true to say that I would never have become a schoolmaster, nor indeed gone to King's College Cambridge, without his influence.

To him also I owe my passionate love of classical music. In the course of my first year in the school, when I only knew him as a terrifying, though inspiring, teacher of History, he had come up to me after one lesson with the following invitation. 'Would you like to come with me to a concert in Brighton?' I had never been to a concert in my life and this clearly showed in my face. He continued, 'If you do not enjoy it I won't ask you again and I can guarantee you a good tea after it.' I can still remember that

Terne House, Summer 1948: Christopher Chamberlin (Housemaster) seated centre; Middle Row (standing) author on left, Peter and Michael Ball on right, brother Richard seated on ground in front of Housemaster.

first concert given by the Southern Philharmonic Orchestra in the Dome in Brighton under the conductor Herbert Menges. Mendelssohn's Overture *The Hebrides*, followed by the Mendelssohn Violin Concerto played by the leader of the orchestra and Beethoven's Seventh Symphony. It was the last work which completely mesmerized me. Yes, the tea was very good but the music remained magic. On our return to the College he invited me in and on finding out what my reaction had been he gave me a set of five 78 rpm records of the Symphony conducted by Toscanini (a spare set, he claimed) which I retained until the LP era came in. And the first 78 I bought myself with carefully saved up pocket money was the overture *The Hebrides* played by the Minneapolis Symphony Orchestra conducted by Rudolph Ganz. More concerts followed over the years – most memorably I still remember a very young Elizabeth Schwarzkopf singing the Richard Strauss Four Last Songs, Solomon playing the Brahms Second Piano Concerto and Shura Cherkassky playing the Dohnanyi *Variations on a Nursery Theme.*

The Director of Music at the College, Jasper Rooper, was an Old Boy of Lancing who was determined on return from evacuation to renew the musical life of the College. He had begun a Concert Club in 1946 and the first recital was given by Peter Pears (OL) and Benjamin Britten. There were six concerts each year and many well known artists of the time came and performed to enthusiastic audiences, amongst them myself. He also organized school trips to the Concert Series in the Dome and conducted a major choral work each year. The three of us were in the school choir and in 1948 at the Centenary of the Foundation had the privilege of leading the procession into Chapel which consisted of 16 bishops (the Lambeth Conference was on at the time).

There were five processions altogether. The first consisted of the representatives of the visiting schools (15 of them) with their banners and the Lancing teaching staff in gowns and hoods with Dr Barbara Russell Wells, the only female member of the

Common Room, resplendent in her crimson doctorate robe. She was a kind and caring person known to the boys as 'Middle Sex'. The second was all the Headmasters and Headmistresses of the Woodard Corporation, the third for Fellows of the four Divisions, those of the Southern Division resplendent in their blue copes. We led the fourth, which was the sixteen visiting bishops. In addition to the English representatives, there were others from Australia, America, Africa and Asia including the Bishop of Korea. The final procession consisted of the Lancing choir, the chaplains of the Southern Division, the Dean of Chichester, the Archdeacons of the Diocese, the four Provosts, the President of the Corporation, Kenneth Kirk the Bishop of Oxford, and finally the Bishop of Chichester as Visitor – the great Bishop George Bell.

The Chapel was full to capacity. There were over 1,000 people present. Much of the music had been specially written for the occasion by Old Boys of the school. It was indeed a memorable occasion, one of many that I remember there.

Nathaniel Woodard is one of the most remarkable figures in education in the nineteenth century. After a brief spell as a curate in Bethnal Green (from which he was removed after an unfortunate sermon in which he preached in favour of the provision in the Prayer Book for confession and absolution and which drew complaints to his bishop) he went to Shoreham by Sea in Sussex as a curate. Here he was made aware of the lack of educational opportunity for the middle classes and was allowed to open a small day school for middle class boys in the dining room of the vicarage. In 1848 he published a pamphlet 'A Plea for the Middle Classes' in which he stressed the need to 'provide a good and complete education for the middle classes at such a charge as will make it available for most of them.' He was proposing that the Church should undertake the task of providing secondary education on a national basis. He drew up a scheme for graded schools to be set up in five areas of the country. His first foundations were Lancing (1848), Hurstpierpoint (1849) and Ardingly (1858). Lancing was to be for the upper middle class and the sons of professional men; Hurstpierpoint, the middle school for 'the sons of tradesmen, farmers, clerks etc.' and Ardingly, the lower school for 'the sons of small shopkeepers, mechanics, clerks, gin palace keepers and the like.'

The fees were to be graded also and indeed it was possible at Ardingly until the First World War for pupils to earn their education by working in the buildings and on the grounds. Woodard even went so far as to say that when the Headmasters travelled by train to a meeting, the Head of Lancing should travel first class, Hurstpierpoint second class and Ardingly third class! Of course, nowadays the schools all charge very similar fees and provide a very similar education but in the mid-nineteenth century this was indeed a remarkable new concept.

And Woodard was expert at putting his views across. He had some powerful supporters in London, including Lord Salisbury, and was an expert and prolific fundraiser. By the time of his death in 1891 he had eight boys' schools and three girls' schools in his Corporation, and had invested half a million pounds in setting them up – a very considerable sum of money for that time. The Woodard Corporation has continued to grow and develop and today there are thirty two schools within it which stretch from Penzance to Tynemouth and embrace all boy, all girl, co-educational, secondary, primary and boarding and day establishments. It is the largest single educational group in the independent school world.

His philosophy is summed up in the words which he left to each member of the St Nicholas Corporation:

Never play the Hero.
Seek to pass through life without attracting the eyes of men.
Slight no man's good opinion, much less his love.
Never challenge the world.
Neither seek nor depend on the praises of men.
Consider the success of the Society to rest on your shoulders solely.
Do all to the sole glory of God.

As Basil Handford, the great Lancing teacher and historian said 'These are precisely the right precepts for a man who felt that he was the involuntary instrument of a divine purpose.'

The masters teaching at Lancing in those immediate post-war years were a remarkable collection of men. The Head of Mathematics, Major Parnell-Smith, was in his late sixties. He was a very small man who always wore stout black boots. He had commanded the Corps at Lancing and had stood as Liberal candidate for the Shoreham by Sea constituency (he saved his deposit). He was a heavy smoker and always used a long cigarette holder. I can remember him now, feet on the desk, the cigarette holder in operation – and when he came to draw a straight line on the blackboard it was unbelievably wavy as his hand shook so much, but he was an outstanding teacher of mathematics. The other mathematician I remember was Marvin Puttock, also well past sixty. He had been born with only one arm of full length but had played cricket when at Lancing as a boy and was reputed to be the only man who had ever hit a ball over the roof of the Chapel from the First XI square – a considerable feat. His 'party trick' was to draw a perfect circle on the blackboard and then throw the chalk over his shoulder – always finding his boy target! He was also an excellent teacher who when he left Lancing went on to Millfield and continued teaching until his eighties. E.B. Gordon, another OL, was a remarkable man. He had been a great athlete but had been injured at school while taking part in the notorious five mile cross country race when he fell in one of the ten dykes (streams) which littered the final mile of the course and injured his back. He was a small, bent figure but devoted to Lancing. On sunny days he would lead his class for a walk in the valley looking for wild flowers and teaching us to love nature. He ran the St Nicholas Press, high up in the Triforium of the Chapel, and it is thanks to him that I am to this day terrified of heights. He had taken two of us up to the press and we then went outside on to the roof of the Chapel. There were warning lights on the apex of the roof for the benefit of planes landing at nearby Shoreham airport and a bulb needed replacing (one of his many tasks). He went up a flying buttress at speed – the walls of it were at about knee height – and called to us to follow. He was by then sitting astride the roof. I foolishly looked down and was frozen with terror. I do not to this day know how I got down but even now cannot face climbing a ladder to any height. He would have been so upset to know the misery I had felt for he was kindness itself.

The Rev. Wilfred Derry was an excellent school Chaplain. He had been Chaplain during the war years and evacuation and did much beyond the duties of chaplaincy. He ran the Book Room, the Scouts, the Model Railway Society and the Estate Club and also organized the Friends of Lancing Chapel and invariably wore scouts shorts and stockings under his cassock. He drove an elderly Rolls Royce which we all greatly admired and, with the Headmaster, was responsible for the very good religious atmosphere in Chapel and school generally. There were two assistant Chaplains, the Rev. W.M. (Moffat) Howitt and the Rev. Henry Thorold. Moffat in 1911 had been a curate in the East End of London, had contracted tuberculosis and was sent to Lancing having been given six months to live – the sea air it was hoped would help him. He bicycled to the sea every morning and swam and by 1945 when I first met him had been at Lancing for 34 years. He was gentleness itself and taught Latin, Greek, French and the violin as well as singing with a very pure tone as alto in the choir. When he left Lancing he became Rector in the little village of Trotton near Midhurst in West Sussex with a beautiful little church with a number of fine brasses. To the astonishment of all who knew him he married late in life a rich American widow and it was a joy to see this dear man who had never had a penny in his life, spilling pound and five pound notes when he took his handkerchief out of his pocket.

The other Chaplain was a real eccentric – the Rev. Henry Thorold. He was also the owner of a fine old Rolls Royce. His first lesson of the year would be spent in asking each boy in each class

Lancing Chapel from the cricket field.

where he lived. He would then state – 'Ah yes, I went there on June 2nd 1941' (as it might be) and if one ever tested him on this a few weeks later he would always produce the same answer. He always taught with his classroom door open 'to see who was coming and to make a quick getaway' and on the blackboard was a statement 'Only sixty one lazy days to the end of the term' – the number was changed each day. There was a fine coloured coat of arms at the bottom of the board and a phrase 'Remove Classics Evening School (Lancing word for prep.) Prose 23' – this never changed throughout the year. He had a very good mind and was an extreme snob. When a Housemaster, his advice to his House tutor was 'Never invite parents to sit down, they never know when to go', but he was a very lively part of the Lancing scene. When he left Lancing he went to his country seat, Marston Hall Lincolnshire, and wrote many contributions to the series of Shell guides to the Counties of England.

The Head of Languages was Dr Ernst Saenger, a German of great scholarship but with no sense of humour. After School Certificate I had decided to study Modern Languages. There were three of us in the Lower Sixth, Christopher Wightwick who became Head of KCS Wimbledon and then an HMI, Alan Alexander who became a prep school Headmaster and myself. We had twenty four lessons a week with the Doctor, twelve for French and twelve for German. He decided that we should attempt the Higher Certificate in one year rather than two and to my astonishment we all passed. The other two were older than I was and left soon after but I was only $16^{1}/_{2}$ and had time to fill in. Of Dr Saenger more will appear later in this narrative.

In the November of 1948 I went at Christopher Chamberlin's suggestion to King's College Cambridge for an interview. The first sight of that Chapel and inspiring front court made me determined to get there. After the long train journey up from Shoreham via London I had 15 minutes with Patrick Wilkinson, the Senior Tutor, which seemed to me to be a pleasant chat about nothing in particular and he then saw me off with the words: 'Well we shall have a place for you here but not until you are over 19, so go back to Lancing and don't do anything naughty for three years!' It was a sombre thought that I was to be at school for another two and a half to three years. I must confess that for the remainder of that academic year I did very little and in Summer 1949 took the Higher Certificate examination again with virtually no improvement on the previous year's marks. Dr Peter Thompson was now in charge of Modern Languages and Harry Meyrick was teaching me German, but after discussions with my Housemaster it was decided that the following year I would take History and English as my main subjects, reverting to Languages in the September 1950 term prior to sitting the Cambridge Scholarship Examination.

Thus I really came to know another really great Lancing eccentric, Patrick Halsey. Patrick was an Old Etonian but never referred to his old school. The only time I ever saw him wear an OE tie was when, in a quartet of masters, he performed 'The Stately Homes of England' – where the line 'The playing fields of Eton have made us frightfully brave' received an extra loud cheer. I had been taught History by him in a lower form and have vivid recollections of him demonstrating how the Egyptians raised their obelisks – as he lay on the floor in his classroom with his head and shoulders over the end of the dais and gradually stood on his head, how he took off his gown and threw it out of the classroom door with a shout of 'export only' and how he got under his desk to demonstrate how a caveman existed in the ancient world. He was in this latter situation when the Headmaster opened the classroom door and said to the assembled form 'Oh I see Mr Halsey is not here at the moment.'

The Sixth Form historians were taught in his study in Field's House and demonstrations went on. I remember how the Grand Staircase of the Imperial Palace was constructed out of a high-backed armchair and various cushions so that we could witness Rasputin, after taking poison, collapsing down the staircase. But from him and my Housemaster I learnt much and it was similar in English with Basil Handford and a newcomer to the staff, Donald Bancroft, who later was to do many adaptations of classic English novels for readings on the BBC.

During these years I had continued to enjoy Lancing to the full. In the Summer holidays of 1948 I had to have an operation on both feet. I had been finding walking more and more difficult and it was decided that all the bones in my toes should be broken and then the feet set in plaster for nine months. My father cut a pair of shoes so that I could put the plaster on the soles and for the whole of that September term I was given a dispensation that I could, if necessary, be late for classes by five minutes. It was a difficult time but everyone was very friendly. When the plaster was finally taken off, the specialist said to me, 'Well, you will be able to walk but I am afraid that there won't be any games. (To me this was the best possible news for one of the few bad memories I have is of hearing comments from my fellows when teams' names went up on the house noticeboard – Oh God, we've got Griffiths again!) However, you will not have to be in a wheelchair, which was a possibility.' No one had told me of that even being a possibility thank goodness.

One offshoot of this was that I received rapid promotion in the CCF. Up until then, I had been a rather lacklustre Lance Corporal but John Alston, the Director of Music who had succeeded Jasper Rooper and who commanded the Corps, decreed that I should be appointed CQMS in charge of the Armoury, under the SM and the BM, the two regular old soldiers who served in the CCF and looked after the shooting. This meant I had a great badge on my sleeve, a scarlet sash and no boots! A cushy 'job' if ever there was one. When I left the College in 1951 there was a queue of volunteers to succeed me but the post was declared redundant. The best feature was the Annual Inspection where my job was to meet the Inspecting Officer and escort him to the CO and thereafter I could be a spectator!

In the Summer holidays of 1949, Harry Meyrick and his great friend, Colin Weir the former Oxford goalkeeper and a History master, invited Christopher Wightwick and myself to go on a camping holiday in France and Germany. I had been abroad before. In 1947 I had been on an exchange to a French family in the fascinating town of Le Puy en Velay. M. Mauriange was the successful owner of a factory that made French clothes. I was presented with a suit in herringbone grey tweed which looked like the Lancing school uniform but which was rejected out of hand on my return to England by my father because it was styled à la française with tight waist. The Mauriange family were very good to me. Each day after breakfast Monsieur sat down with a map and planned an outing to show me the countryside. An essential feature was to arrive at a good restaurant at midday. The kitchens were inspected, the meal ordered for 1.00 p.m., then a little sightseeing followed by two to two and a half hours of food (and drink for the adults) and then back home for a siesta! I had a wonderful fortnight and then back to Wales with André. My brother Richard had just acquired two pairs of boxing gloves (goodness knows why). André had been in our home for twenty minutes only when he succeeded in knocking Richard out cold, which did not endear him to my mother, but the visit was reasonably successful despite a total lack of French from my parents.

The following year Richard and I were entrusted to Messrs Thomas Cook to go on a week's visit to Paris. We stayed in a small hotel with the splendid name of the Hotel de l'Univers et Portugal! My main memories of this are visits to Versailles and Fontainebleau and then one miraculous evening to the opera at the Palais Garnier. It was my first visit to an opera, *La Traviata*, with a young up and coming singer called Maria Callas, and I can still remember it now. It was the first of many nights at the opera over the next few years.

So now we were off in Harry Meyrick's old Austin Ten. The first stop was at Rheims at the Chateau d'Harcourt. The old Count was a friend of Harry's and we pitched our tents on the lawn outside the Chateau. The main disadvantage of the visit from our point of view was that Christopher and I were sat down after breakfast each morning to do some French translation (the Count's idea). The family owned a champagne vineyard and we visited that and the Cathedral in the city. Then after three days it was on to Lake Como where we pitched our tents beside the lake and suffered a major thunderstorm with much lightning. Then we went over the St Gotthard pass. The old car was finding it difficult so it was decided by the other three, that I should walk up to the top where they and the car would wait for me – and that is what happened! It was a truly wonderful three weeks – the only two disasters being when we camped on a stretch of beach beside the Rhine and pitched our tents on sand which was totally flooded as the river rose in the night, and the other when an alpine cow stood on the running board of the car which broke off and had to be tied on the roof for the remainder of the journey. One good result of the flooding was a unanimous decision that for the remainder of the holiday we would find B&Bs or small hotels – which meant comfort, warmth and better food, if more expensive.

But back to Lancing College. In the Spring of 1948 my brother Richard sat the Scholarship Entrance examination. He won the top scholarship and came into the school in the Summer term. It was the custom in those days for scholars to enter in the second form, the Remove, so in September 1948 at the age of 13.2 he found himself in the School Certificate form. Having passed that with flying colours he entered the Lower Sixth in September 1949 at the age of 14.2 and joined the Modern Language VIth. I think this reveals one of the weaknesses of the educational system at the time. It was a very limited education – in my own case in my first term at Lancing, Sam Jagger had said to me 'Greek, German or Science?' and having taken German at Lickey Hills I chose that. Thus for one year I had one lesson a week of Science, Chemistry the first term, Physics in the Lent term and Biology in the Summer term and thereafter none. Richard's education was similarly limited. Thank goodness nowadays they do not rush the brighter pupils through the school but give everyone at least the basis of a good broad education.

The Modern Language VI was small and so the years tended to be banded together for most class periods. I thus found myself working alongside a brother who was $3^{1}/_{2}$ years younger and having to defend him against my older contemporaries who, not unnaturally, resented being outclassed by one so much younger than they were. But he – and I – survived.

That Christmas term Peter and Michael Ball left the school. Peter by then had become Head Boy and Michael was Head of House and I was one of the House Prefects. Our House Matron, Audrey Irby, was a great music lover and we were often invited in for coffee and biscuits before retiring to bed in order to hear the latest LP she had acquired. These were a very new and exciting invention then and of course I longed to acquire a collection of my own. For the present, however, it was still the era of 78s and my collection of these was growing, concertos and symphonies purchased one record at a time, as I managed to save some money out of my weekly pocket money.

Other memories of Lancing still persist. In view of my totally limited athletic ability, Christopher Chamberlin, who most expertly and successfully ran the athletics, co-opted me into helping with them as a timekeeper and measurer of field events. I spent many happy days, therefore, on the athletics field without the ignominy of having to participate and fail publicly. The cross country course at Lancing is nearly six miles long. It begins on the downs above the College and the last mile is down in the valley – the dyke field. Dykes were streams or ditches filled with water which the local farmer had cut across his fields – they were about five feet across and two to three feet of water deep – and at the end of a long run they were nigh on impossible to jump across. There were some 10 of them and so the cross country course meant a wet and cold end to every race. Part of the fun for me as a timekeeper was the race to various parts of the course in either Wilfred Derry's or Sheppard Frere's vintage Rolls Royce to cheer on (and time) the runners. These two cars were magnificent machines and were the inspiration for me when I came in 1957 to purchase my first car (a 1933 20/25 Park Ward Rolls Royce saloon.)

I had also become interested in amateur dramatics. The stage at Lancing in those days was the dais in Great School with curtains put up and very little room for manoeuvre, but my first venture on to the boards was a minor role in Marlowe's *Doctor Faustus*. There was to be much more dramatic involvement later in my first teaching post at Charterhouse.

In 1950, Christopher Chamberlin had invited the Provost of his old College, King's Cambridge to come to Lancing to speak to the Sixth Form. Sir John Sheppard was a remarkable man. In the

Memoir, which the College published about him on his death for old members of the College, the author, Patrick Wilkinson, wrote of him as follows:

> It is a hopeless task to attempt to convey, particularly to anyone who knew him only in his later years, the extraordinary character of Sir John Sheppard, Lecturer in Classics at King's from 1908 to 1933, Vice-Provost from 1929 to 1933, and Provost for the twenty-one years 1933 to 1954 – the attraction of his personality; the almost hypnotic power of those slightly protruding eyes, which could have been sinister had it not been so patently benevolent; the dignity wilfully varied with clowning; the histrionics and rhetoric; the splendid sense of humour and fun; the shrewdness streaked with naiveté; the constitutional toughness masquerading as senile debility; the inexhaustible interest in people and desire to help them; the egoism which yet did good by stealth; the total devotion to the College which was yet an extension of the ego; and the paternal hold established on it, such that after nineteen years the Fellows unanimously prolonged his tenure of the Provostship for two years beyond the normal retiring age. It may be doubted whether in the five hundred years of its existence any man so imposed his personality on it, though he was essentially carrying on and intensifying humane traditions which it had already acquired through others.

His lecture was spellbinding. Again I quote from the Memoir:

> He never used notes, even when nearly eighty years old, he gave three [lectures] in one day at Stockton-on-Tees. There is a story that when an effusive young woman came up after a lecture and begged to borrow his notes, he fumbled about and found an envelope which had scribbled on it 'Zeus-Agamemnon-Zeus'. This must surely be apocryphal, for he never needed so much. He had great rhetorical gifts – with his long white hair he inevitably recalled Lloyd George; but a still greater asset was his dramatic power. When he lectured on Homer or tragedy he could become each character in turn, now reproducing the actual words, in Greek or English, now a paraphrase. He did not imitate, but you

accepted him as Antigone at one moment, as Creon at the next. He was thus able to convey to an audience the feeling of witnessing the drama, not merely being told about it, while having it interpreted at the same time – and it is doubtful if anyone else in England was able to do that. It was useless to try to take notes, and you could rarely remember afterwards much of what he said; but when he was in good form you retained a feeling that you had been participating in something infinitely worthwhile, and an inspiration to go and read the text or see the play. Sometimes you would also have been hilariously entertained, at the expense perhaps of some misguided scholar who doubted whether one man had composed the Homeric poems entire.

When A.E. Houseman first came to Cambridge in 1911 he said to Sheppard, 'I hear your lectures are very well attended, so I know they must be bad'. It is true that he was at his best with a popular audience, ranging from Hellenic Travellers on a cruise or a local branch of the Classical Association to a rotary club or a girls' school. The more unlikely the audience, the greater the challenge and reward, as when he spellbound a society of Clare athletes with a talk on the *Agamemnon*. He would establish rapport by a gimmick of some kind, sitting on a table perhaps and swinging his legs, his long pants showing between his trousers and boots. As *The Times* obituarist put it, 'As he warmed to his work, especially if he felt his audience to be with him, he would perch on chair or desk in postures of ever more perilous disequilibrium, which continually threatened a disaster that never came.' Of course his audience was not *always* with him, and there were not a few, especially in academic circles, who looked askance at such antics.

After his talk, back in Teme House, I was introduced to him as one who hoped to come to King's and certainly after meeting him and listening to him there was nowhere else I wanted to go.

My last term at Lancing I was Head of House and a School Prefect and I much enjoyed working closely with the Headmaster, for whom I retained and retain the highest respect. There was then a summer spent in France and Barry and up to Cambridge in October 1951.

The previous December I had been to Cambridge to sit for the Scholarship Entrance examinations. I had reverted to life as a Modern Language specialist in preparation for this. It was a great experience. There were some sixty or so of us staying in King's and it was interesting to note the different approach to the examination of boys from different educational backgrounds. Those of us from independent schools tended to relax outside the examination room, particularly in the evenings after dinner. The grammar school representatives had large numbers of books with them and revised constantly. They certainly showed some of us up and had more success in gaining Scholarships! I was, however, fortunate to be given a place on the strength of what I had produced in my papers and at interview. The most memorable event was meeting the Provost, Sir John Sheppard. Having met him on his visit to Lancing I knew what to expect – some of the other candidates did not! We were invited some ten at a time to the Provost's Lodge where we were sat on the floor in a circle. Sir John went round talking to each one individually and then from a large armchair entertained us for an hour with reminiscences about King's. Although he was not officially an examiner, it was said that when the examiners were meeting to consider which candidates were being admitted he showed a personal knowledge of many of them and was the cause of some being admitted to the College whose written work might well have precluded them.

Chapter 4

AFTER THE ENTRANCE EXAMINATIONS it was decided that I would spend one further term at Lancing. That Lent term 1951 was a great joy. I had my place at Cambridge, I was now Head of Teme House (for sadly Peter and Michael had left the school), there was little need for work and I would really enjoy those aspects of school which appealed. I was a School Librarian which gave me a love of books which remains to this day. I was School Sacristan which gave me a firm foundation for my Christian belief, which I retain to this day; I was involved with the Modern Language, Play Reading, Debating and Gramophone Societies, all interests which I have retained throughout my life. I learnt from my Housemaster some of those skills so very necessary for dealing with other people and I learnt from my Headmaster some of the pleasures (and indeed some of the problems) of leadership.

Leaving school is a strange experience. Throughout my life to that moment I had been a part of a community. I now found myself in a small town in South Wales where I knew virtually no contemporaries, where my father was in his office five days a week, with a mother who because of her agoraphobia, did not wish to leave the house. At my father's suggestion I took up playing bowls. My feet were certainly better after my operation and of course in bowls one can sit down during the game (unless it is a singles match). I found to my great joy that for the first time in my life I was actually succeeding at a game. Bowls is essentially a sociable game, even in the competitive atmosphere of tournament play. I suppose to succeed at it requires a blend of a good eye, the skill of concentration and a fair amount of luck. There were one or two other younger members of the Bowling

41

Club but on the whole I was playing with contemporaries of my father and grandfather – and a splendid bunch of men they were. I played in the team on a Saturday and that first summer won the Club Handicap competition. In August I was asked if I would like to go on tour with the club to the Bideford area of the country. My abiding memory of this was arriving at one club where our captain was told that their oldest member would like to play five ends against our youngest as 'that was what kept him going throughout the year'. As I was the youngest by some 40 years I went on to the green. A little old gentleman came to join me and I was soundly beaten by him. As we left the green he asked me how old I thought he was. I hazarded that he might be in his late eighties. 'I am in my hundredth year,' he replied. There cannot be many sports where an age difference of 100-19 can make no difference to the standard of competition and it was certainly a lesson for me.

On our return the family left, as usual, for the annual visit to Llandrindod Wells and I played for the first time in the tournament, though without great success. Then a short trip to Paris and it was time to set off for Cambridge.

At King's at that time it was the custom for first year undergraduates who were not scholars to be out in lodgings for their first year. I found to my initial horror that I was to be at 120 Vinery Road which turned out to be a 15 minute bus ride from the College in the centre of Cambridge. My mother, in an excess of matriarchal care, had never allowed my brother and myself to have bicycles and so it was to be a year of public transport. But what a year! Mr and Mrs Smith at whose house I found myself, had never had a lodger before but their son, Peter, had recently married and left home and I found myself welcomed as one of the family. Mrs Smith spoilt me completely, doing all my laundry, cooking me splendid meals and generally mothering me. Mr Smith was a remarkable man. He was a pharmaceutical dispenser at Boots in the centre of the city and was one of the best-read men I have ever come across. He was interested in everything and had a very wide general knowledge. When I left them after a very happy first year we kept in touch and Mrs Smith lived long enough to see the birth of my first daughter in 1966.

King's was a very remarkable College. The buildings are of course magnificent. It was a small College as far as numbers went with, in those days, some 240 undergraduates with 80+ Fellows. One of its unusual features was the way in which dons and undergraduates would queue up for lunch together and sit together on the benches at the tables in the great Dining Hall. Thus one might find oneself sitting next to the Provost, the Vice-Provost Professor Adcock, the great University Librarian Schofield, Professor Pigou, one's own tutor or even E.M. Forster who had been elected an Honorary Fellow in 1945 and lived in the College. The conversation would flow and it was very satisfying for us to see these great men eating the same lunch as we ourselves. (The food actually was pretty good.)

I was reading Modern Languages and my tutors were Donald Beves for French and Humphrey Trevelyan for German in that first year. Donald had gone down from King's in 1922 and became a Clerk in the House of Commons which gave him enough time and leisure to write a thesis on The Holy Grail in Early French Poetry. This won him his Fellowship and he returned to King's in September 1924. From then onwards until his death in 1961 he became one of the best loved and most influential members of the College. He spent any leisure time in acting and collecting the finest private collection of Stuart and Georgian glass of the time, which was beautifully displayed in his rooms down near the river. The collection went, on his death, to the Fitzwilliam Museum in Cambridge. He would invite all his pupils to dine in his rooms once a year, six at a time, and would delight in using some of the collection on these occasions, to the education but also alarm of the recipients.

As an actor he was a supreme Shakespearian comic but his

comic powers extended far beyond Shakespeare. He was excellent in Molière and gave reality and truth to lightweight comedy such as Noel Coward. He also thoroughly enjoyed himself in revue sketches and the ballards of Victorian music hall. He took part in the Marlowe Society recordings for the British Council of the whole Shakespeare canon. He also read aloud beautifully and will long be remembered for his readings in the service of Nine Lessons and Carols from King's at Christmas.

To be tutored by Donald was a great experience. He would sit in silence as I read my weekly essay, would then take it, put his monocle in place and then after a few moments let it drop from his eye with the comment, 'Pas mal. Now have you been to the theatre this week?' Tutorials were to teach one about the good things of life and so a discussion of the latest play at the Arts Theatre or in London, followed by a consideration of any exhibition on in Cambridge, followed by a glass of the most excellent dry sherry or dry white wine was the usual form. He certainly prepared his pupils for life as much as for examinations.

Another pupil of his, Dr Robert Bolgar, who also became a don at King's and incidentally also tutored me in my second and third years, wrote the following of him:

> Donald did not so much teach as encourage undergraduates to show off their little learning. He never 'lectured' in supervisions and seemed to avoid lengthy explanations. But he was remarkably acute in spotting errors, which he would correct by saying just enough to make one understand what was wrong and why. His appreciative listening, his reluctance to hold forth in his turn and his telling criticisms combined to produce a strange result. One was tempted to feel cleverer than this unassuming man who seemed averse from making an effort, and yet one was afraid to yield to this temptation being sure that one would be caught out.
>
> His technique of correction rather than explanation worked best in Part I language teaching. In Part II it was most helpful with the constitutionally inaccurate, and with the clever but muddled

who did not express their ideas clearly. His lectures were pleasantly delivered, and were a lucid, detailed exposition of what was generally held to be true on the topic he was discussing.

In the last analysis the content of what he taught was unimportant for him and for us. Imparting information about the French language and French literature, and collecting a store of specialized knowledge about the sixteenth century, was the job he had chosen, and his self-respect was deeply involved in doing this job well. But there his concern stopped. He did not feel that what he taught could or should affect his students in any deeper sense. And he was right. What mattered for us was not Donald the thinker, but Donald the man, who was modest without being in any sense weak, and who managed to be gentle and kindly without sacrificing his standards.

It was the same with supervision in research. He left the pupil to form his own ideas and collect the facts. It was only then that he asked to see the results in writing. His contribution was to see through any faulty argument, and particularly to improve presentation and English style.

I count it a great privilege to have been taught by Donald and to have considered him a friend. Humphrey Trevelyan, the son of the great historian, G.M. Trevelyan, was a sound German Scholar and a very nice man. He would have been an outstanding schoolmaster and I had a very good year as his pupil.

I made particular friends with five other members of the College – Colin Harris and Roger Clark, two Old Carthusians, Colin Nears from Ipswich Grammar School and Philip Oswald and Nicholas Temperley who were Old Etonians. None of us was a games player but King's in fact was at that time not a particularly 'sporting' College. We shared interests in music and the theatre and there was plenty of both in Cambridge and with occasional visits to London. After a few months we decided that instead of lunching in College hall we would take it in turns on weekdays to provide lunch for the six of us. This continued throughout our time in Cambridge. On one occasion during our second year, one of the dons stopped me in the front Court. 'I hear you have your own little lunch club,' he said. 'You might care to have this, it needs two hours in boiling water,' and he handed me a parcel. Back in my room I opened it – it was a haggis! At 11.00 a.m. I put it on the stove; at noon I went out to buy the rest of lunch. On my return my room was in chaos. I did not know that a haggis, like sausages, should be perforated with a fork before cooking. There were now pieces of haggis on the ceiling, walls, floor and furniture which took several hours to clean up! But usually lunches proceeded calmly.

At the end of the year when Part I exams had just finished, I received a letter from John Dancy, the new Headmaster of Lancing. One of the modern language staff was ill and he wondered if I would stand in for a month. It was a great opportunity and I seized it. On arrival at Lancing the thing which impressed me most was the fact that some of those who had taught me and whom I had considered old men were in fact only five to ten years older than I was. This was brought home to me in the classroom after about a week. I had taught a class of 15 year olds – I was then just over 20 myself. At the end of the lesson, one very serious young pupil stopped me as I was leaving the classroom. 'Excuse me, Sir, you were at Lancing weren't you?' 'Yes indeed'. 'I wonder, Sir, were you here with my father?'

In general though this teaching was a great experience and convinced me that I had chosen the right profession. On my fifteenth birthday my father had asked me what I wanted to be when I grew up. I had replied immediately 'a schoolmaster' (the influence of Lancing already). There was a silence and he then said: 'All right. I will see you through Cambridge and then it is over to you'. On my brother's fifteenth birthday, he was asked the same question and replied ' a university professor' and received the same answer as I had. It was only some twenty years later when I was already Headmaster of Hurstpierpoint College and my brother was a don and Dean of Selwyn College Cambridge that my father said to us: 'I was so disappointed that neither of you wanted to come into and eventually take over the practice I had founded but I must confess that I am now very proud of you both.' How lucky we were to have such a father. I have known many people whose fathers have insisted that they should follow his profession and sadly often with disastrous results and disappointment.

During that month at Lancing I was fortunate enough to pay the first of many visits to Glyndebourne to the opera house. It happened as follows. I was walking through the College when I met Esther Neville-Smith, the widow of a fine schoolmaster who had taught me when I was a pupil at Lancing. She was a great music lover and was, in fact, responsible for persuading Benjamin Britten to write his Cantata *St Nicholas* for the centenary in 1948. 'Can you borrow a dinner jacket for this evening?' she asked me. 'I have a spare ticket for Glyndebourne this evening and we are going with Ben and Peter.' I said yes please and had a wonderful time including a superb picnic with her and Peter Pears and Benjamin Britten, who both glowed about the opera *Alceste* by Glück, a composer of whom I had not heard at that date!

My second year at King's was uneventful apart from one success. All Modern Linguists were expected to enter for the Modern Language French Literature prize which that year was to translate into French an essay from E.M. Forster's book *Two Cheers for Democracy*. I have always enjoyed translation work into French and as this essay included some lines of poetry I managed to produce some correctly rhyming Alexandrine verse. I won the prize, part of which was to take tea with E.M. Forster himself. He was a very shy but delightful person who ended the session by presenting me with a copy of his book which he had signed. I also received 5 calf-bound volumes of French classical literature with a gold embossed King's crest on their front covers.

At the end of my first year I had taken examinations for Part 1 of the Modern Language Tripos in French and German and had gained a not very distinguished II 2 degree. I had never enjoyed

German as much as French and therefore had decided only to take French in Part II of the degree. For 16th Century, I was to study with Donald Beves and for 17th, 18th, 19th and 20th Century with Dr Robert Bolgar. I was used to Donald and his civilized way of imparting knowledge not just of the French subject in hand but of life and civilization itself. Robert Bolgar was a very different tutor. An extremely intelligent and imaginative scholar, he was a very hard taskmaster. The study of each century was the same. We took an author per fortnight, during which I was expected to read a major proportion of that author's output and produce an essay. This was a straightforward approach with a writer who had produced one or two major works, with an author such as Balzac with an immense output of long novels it meant an incredible amount of reading – fortunately I have always been a quick reader! It was an exhausting year but an exhilarating one.

I had moved in from Vinery Road and now had rooms in the King's annexe adjacent to the Arts Theatre. It was pleasant to be in the centre of Cambridge though I missed the cosseting of Mr and Mrs Smith. Our lunch group continued to meet and we enjoyed life. There was plenty of music and I had been invited to join COI (Consolidated Operas Incorporated), a society in King's, which met once a fortnight to sing through various operas and operettas. The main roles were, of course, taken by Choral Scholars, the music was played (at one keyboard) by Boris Ord, the Director of Music at King's, and Philip Radcliffe, a shy and retiring music don. They played from a full orchestral score and their styles of playing were splendidly contrasted. Boris sat back from the keyboard and played with great brio, Philip had his nose just above the keys and played with great skill but no display whatsoever. They were happy and instructive evenings.

There were concerts in the University and also in the City, usually in one of the cinemas there. Colin Davis and the Chelsea Opera Group came each year and were a great joy. The LPO came annually with a conductor who went on to become a celebrity conductor of the Cleveland Orchestra in the USA, George Szell. Of course at that stage we had no idea that these were some of the great men of the future in world music. The vivid memory I have is of meeting the pianist Solomon in Donald Beves' rooms. Donald was at the time taking a major role in a play in Cambridge, Solomon had just performed a superb piano recital of four Beethoven Sonatas (without a score of course). As he came in to the room, his opening words were: 'Donald, I cannot imagine how you remember all those words', which was intriguing in view of his memory for notes as he had just demonstrated.

There were the occasional visits to Covent Garden and I can vividly remember Rimsky Korsakov's *The Golden Cockerel* and *Die Walkure* from Wagner's Ring. Looking back on it I can now appreciate just how fortunate I was. In December 1952 my parents came up to London and we celebrated my twenty-first birthday with a visit to Flanders and Swann followed by a wonderful dinner at Simpsons in the Strand with my five particular friends and brother Richard present. Preliminary Part II examinations in the summer of 1953 were marked by the fact that we actually had an examination on the day of the Queen's Coronation, which we all felt was a bit hard.

The Summer Holidays were a disaster as my mother was going through a period of deep depression. She would not go out, would not have anyone in and would not be left alone. My father was busy as usual and then was away on bowling business – a tour, the International Competitions and home team matches – so I was at home to look after mother. It was a very wearing time and there was no let up. I went back to Cambridge at the beginning of October in a very depressed state myself and some two weeks into the term had a slight breakdown. The College doctor put me onto some form of drug that made me far worse and for about a month I was incapable of work or really anything. Fortunately I then recovered but it was an unpleasant time which I would never want to repeat.

1957 – A successful year of bowls.

The final year from then onwards was relatively peaceful and once the final exams were over we could enjoy May Week and the delight of the King's May Ball which went on all night, ending with breakfast at about 7.00 a.m. It was E.M. Forster in a speech at the Founder's Feast in King's in 1952 who took as his theme 'Who owns the College?' He concluded that it was the Third Year; and further, that the College consisted of all the Third Years there had ever been. He said: 'In my first year I wasn't sure of my clothes; in my second year I was too sure of myself. In my third year I was just right, without arrogance and with exultation, with occasional song and dance, I owned the place. I know that other Third Year men had felt the same and would feel the same in the future.' I think that he has hit the mark absolutely.

I now had a splendid set of rooms on the first floor in Webb's Court in the College itself. It was situated next to the Provost's Lodge and every so often at about ten o'clock at night there would be a scrabbling at the door and there would be Provost Sheppard. 'Come and have a cup of tea, dear boy,' and we would go into the Lodge where he would hold forth, with much puffing of pipe, on a variety of topics. At about 12-12.30 a.m. one ventured to say, 'I think Mr Provost I should be going now.' The response was usually, 'I have been waiting for you to say that for the last half hour.' But it was not really meant and they were memorable occasions. The year passed far too quickly and in the June I went down with a feeling of sadness – it had been a memorable part of my life.

Chapter 5

THE LONG VACATION passed quickly as usual. I played a lot of bowls and my first game for a County side, Glamorgan. A few weeks touring in France and then it was time for Llandrindod once again.

In October 1954 I went up to New College Oxford. Provost Sheppard had some years before set up with Warden Alec Smith of New College, what they called the Amicabilis Concordia, whereby a number of graduates were exchanged for a year or more. I had decided to sit for the Diploma of Education and as my brother Richard was about to appear at King's having won a Scholarship there, I felt it was in both our interests to be apart! New College was very different from King's though it had an equally warm atmosphere between dons and members of the College. My Cambridge BA entitled me to the status of senior member of the College and gained me an Honorary Oxford BA. I was in lodgings in the High Street near Magdalen Bridge and to my delight found a very congenial Lancing contemporary, Martin Marriott, at New College who introduced me to a new circle of friends.

The Department of Education was in Norham Gardens in North Oxford and there I went each day. I found most of the lectures indescribably boring – the Theory of Education is something that has never greatly interested me and even the 'teaching of Modern Languages' which began with the words: 'What you must always remember, ladies and gentlemen, is that French must always be fun' – though how one makes French irregular verbs fun over a period of time with a group of pupils who have no wish or inclination to learn, baffled me then, and would, I think, baffle me now. In discussions among ourselves I found myself in a decided minority who hoped to teach in independent schools and found also that it was perhaps wiser not to mention that fact too frequently – and certainly not to those who were instructing us. Nevertheless, after one term it was a great joy to think that for the Lent Term one was actually going to be in a school and really learning what it was like.

I was extremely fortunate in that I learnt that my practice term as a student master was to be at Westminster School in London. On arrival there in Dean's Yard I found to my surprise that my Head of Department was to be none other than Ernst Saenger, who had moved there from Lancing. The Modern Language Department were very friendly in their reception of me. Dr Hugo Garten, a great German scholar and opera lover, was a fascinating speaker, particularly when reminiscing of operas he had seen, heard and loved. His three favourites were Wagner's *Die Meistersinger von Nuremburg*, Richard Strauss' *Ariadne auf Naxos* and Verdi's *Falstaff* and his tales of the great singers of the past he had heard in them whetted the appetite. It is interesting that all three have become very favourite operas of mine also. Francis Rawes, a Housemaster, who went on to become Headmaster of St Edmund's School Canterbury, was a great person from whom to learn some of the 'tricks of the trade' and the other members of the Department were equally helpful and encouraging.

I became particularly friendly with John Carleton, the Master of the Queen's Scholars, who was later to become Headmaster of Westminster. He was an Old Boy of the school who wrote a small history of it, which is very readable. He delighted in telling of how the day after its publication he received a copy of the book from his mother with a note to say that she understood it had just come out and he might like a copy! He relished also the story that the summer after it was published, he was on holiday in the Highlands. Seeing a bookshop in a small town he went in and asked the proprietor 'Have you a copy of *The History of Westminster School* which has just come out? It is by a John Carleton'. The reply was, 'And you'll be Mr Carleton, I'm thinking.' 'Why do you say that?' added John. 'Why, who else would be asking for it?'

One of John's customs was to give a drinks party each Sunday morning after the Service in the Abbey for anyone he knew who might be there. I was fortunate enough to attend a number of these and met some remarkably interesting people, ranging from Mrs Neville Chamberlain to Yehudi Menuhin.

The Headmaster, Walter Hamilton, was in my opinion, one of the great Headmasters of the twentieth century. There are so many people still alive who have their own vivid memories of and stories about him. Someone once asked him if he was an optimist or a pessimist. To their surprise he replied: 'An optimist.' 'Why then do you always seem so gloomy?' 'Because I know my optimism is not justified.'

I would like to quote a passage from the introduction to the volume *Walter Hamilton: A Portrait*.

> His mind was not only acute: it was also orderly. Brains he had and moral force too. This also was not much on display: high prating was not his line. But the brief sentence 'It won't do' marked a clear recognition of right and wrong. The Americans have a phrase which says of someone that he worries more about the sizzle than about the steak. Walter was the exact opposite. His Christian faith was communicated to boys without any religiosity: they felt that belief must be intellectually and emotionally respectable if someone of Walter's calibre was sure that it mattered and yet treated it undemonstratively and, when necessary, with humour. All this made him a man to be trusted. You might not actually go tiger-shooting with him, for such pursuits would not be to his taste, but he was certainly a man to have at your side if tigers uninvited were to gather round.
>
> Yet (this indeed is the place for an 'At enim' if you learnt Latin prose with Walter) intelligence, system and moral certainty might be held to be a mark of many headmasters. Walter had a much more individual gift – a style that is well remembered by those who knew him. Some have compared this style to that of Eeyore,

but this does not fully cover it. There was the deep voice; the accent that was not redolent of Oxbridge; the low and even timbre of his speech, which could have seemed monotonous but for the character which underlay it; the expression of inspissated gloom; the curious way of looking up at you, which some (from Socratic memory) likened to that of a bull, but which was in fact gentler – more reminiscent of a heifer disturbed while softly grazing; and, very occasionally, the passionate outburst of anger, cold and hollow in tone.

All this formed an engaging counterpoint to his warm and amusing personality. He had a strong sense of the absurd, and could mock himself readily. There was ripe laughter at his own jokes and those of others ('t...t...t...' was the sound it usually made). He had what one novelist has described as an instinct for the irresponsible playfulness of conversation. During such conversation, his pipe would be endlessly lit, and the smoke of quiet contentment would curl up to the ceiling. Here was company which not only entertained you but also created the strong feeling that, beneath the frivolity, you had someone of weight on your side.'

The boys found him sympathetic. As an article in the *Evening Standard* wrote: 'They imitated his voice. They are still imitating it. It is a good voice to imitate. It is low, deep, melancholy and yet nasal. He could dub a depressed bloodhound for a cartoon film admirably.'

This was the Headmaster for whom I was to work for that Lent Term 1955. After some six or seven weeks he said to me: 'I suppose I ought to come and hear you teach.' We arranged it for the next day. I got the class all prepared and he did not turn up. When I saw him in the Common Room, he said: 'Sorry. I forgot. I'll come tomorrow.' He duly turned up and sat at the back of the class. I was teaching French. After some five minutes, he got up and lumbered out. As he passed my desk he mumbled something incomprehensible. In some trepidation I went up to him later in the Common Room to confess that I had not heard what he had said to me. 'All I said was – I can't understand a word that you are saying, so I am going.'

My first lesson at the school had certainly been unnerving. It was with the Modern Language Seventh, a group of eight extremely intelligent boys, two of them French and two German and all eight of whom gained Oxbridge places. We were to read and study a Racine play. At the start of this first lesson I asked them how they usually studied such a work as I did not wish to alter their methods of study. I said: 'Do you usually read a whole act and then discuss, or a whole scene or have a discussion after each major speech?' They had a little exchange of comments and then the spokesman said: 'There is a bit of a controversy here, Sir, I am afraid. Half of us aim at perfection and the other half, reality.' I still hope that they did not see the panic I felt that I could not even understand what he meant. The thought went through my mind that this was probably the end of a promising career, however, I survived and we discussed the play scene by scene!

One day I found to my horror that I was down to referee a junior leagues game of football. Westminster School being situated in the centre of London has its First XI ground in nearby Vincent Square but most games take place at Grove Park, a twenty minute train ride from Charing Cross railway station. After lunch we assembled the boys in the school yard and handed out bus fares with the order to meet up at Charing Cross in 20 minutes time. There were three of us involved, French, a very keen sporting type and Denis Moylan, a quiet, scholarly, non-athlete like myself. On the train I confessed to Denis that I was ignorant of most of the rules. 'Just follow my example and do as I do,' he replied. The three games started simultaneously. After some 17 minutes Denis whistled for half-time, so I followed suit. Some 15 minutes later he blew for time and hurried off the field indicating to me that I should do the same. As we left the playing fields we heard French whistling for half-time in his match! On the return journey Denis said with some satisfaction: 'We should be just in time for tea,' as

indeed we were on our return to central London. I was not asked
to referee again!

I was in digs in South Audley Street. Wilfred Derry had been
dismissed as Chaplain at Lancing by John Dancy who thought he
had too many extra-chapel commitments (a sad loss to Lancing's
religious life.) and Wilfred had become Priest-in-Charge at the
Grosvenor Chapel. The Rectory was a large house near to the
church and he had four of us ex-Lancing boys lodging there at a
very modest rent. We took it in turns to serve for him at Mass on
Sunday. As the vestry was right next to our dining room, Sunday
lunch was always eaten in a haze of incense which had filtered in
from the vestry. Another task was to take a printed card with details
of each month's services to the reception desks of the large hotels
situated in Park Lane, which gave us some indication of how 'the
other half lived'.

My walk to school each morning took me through Shepherd
Market, across Green Park and St James' Park to Westminster and
back each evening – not perhaps as safe a journey these days as it
was in 1955. It was the cause of another amusing incident with
Denis Moylan. I had invited him back to tea in South Audley
Street and as we walked through Shepherd Market he was
horrified to hear me exchange greetings with some of the French
girls, who in those days plied their wares on the street corners.
Passing through each day as I did, I had got to know (by sight) a
number of them. Denis, a gentle, somewhat prim, bachelor was
appalled by my behaviour and spoke of it – to much general
amusement – in the Common Room the following morning.

Our housekeeper at the Grosvenor Chapel was Florence
Woodard, granddaughter of the founder of Lancing. She was an
eccentric character who looked after us well but ruled us with a
rod of iron. There were many vagrants who knocked at the door
begging for food each day and it was her custom to direct them
immediately round the corner to the Roman Catholic church in
Farm Street! On one occasion she answered the doorbell and from

within the house we heard a loud voice exclaim: 'Good God, Flo, I thought you were dead'. It turned out to be her brother, Canon Alfred Woodard, of whom more will be told later in this memoir.

Term ended and I prepared with some sadness to leave Westminster and return to Oxford. It had been a great experience teaching at such an academically prestigious school and with a group of such intelligent and sociable colleagues. I had also had the chance to make many visits to the opera, theatre and to the then very new Royal Festival Hall. Some concerts remain still in my memory. Edwin Fischer, the great German pianist, gave two concerts in which he played the five Beethoven Concertos and the Triple Concerto, conducting them from the keyboard and in the first four concertos improvising cadenzas on the night – two magnificent evenings. Then Sir Thomas Beecham conducted a concert in memory of Wilhelm Furtwängler at which Jascha Heifetz played the Brahms Violin Concerto. These were but three of many memorable occasions.

I was leaving Dean's Yard for, I thought, the last time when I met the Headmaster. As I went to thank him for having me in his school, he said: 'I have just heard that Hugo Garten has to go into hospital for an operation. Can you come and teach here for the Summer Term?' Delighted, I said yes of course I could and would. I went back to Oxford for the final week of term and went to see Maurice Jacks, the Director of the Department of Education. I told him of the great opportunity this was for me as I wished to make my career in independent schools and assured him that I would nevertheless do all my work and come to Oxford each week for a tutorial. To my dismay he said immediately: 'No way do you leave this course half-way through it.' And that was the end of the interview.

I went back to New College to my tutor to ask what I could do. He suggested that I should speak to the Warden, Alec Smith, as I was in such a dilemma. The Warden listened to my tale and then picked up the telephone. He waved me out of the room but as I left I heard the words: 'The Vice Chancellor wishes to speak to the Director of Education'. Some fifteen minutes later I was summoned back into his study. 'I have persuaded Mr Jacks that it is in your interest to go to Westminster but for goodness sake, work hard and make sure you pass the wretched exams!' On my return to the Department I was summoned to the Director's office where a furious Director declared: 'I was overruled. You may go to Westminster.' And so in the summer I returned to Dean's Yard.

I enjoyed the teaching – Hugo Garten's timetable had been re-arranged so that I did not have much German to teach. I was happy with French at any level. He was master-in-charge of swimming, so I was expected to take this on. I went to see him in hospital to express my worries. 'No problem,' he replied, 'the boys all think that I swam in the 1936 Olympics. To tell you the truth, I cannot swim.' He then gave me some useful advice which included a certain amount of bluff. It meant that three afternoons a week after lunch I lined up a class in Dean's Yard, issued bus money and then met the boys at the public baths in Buckingham Palace Road. To be fair to them, the boys behaved well and did not let me down, though I found taking the team to matches at other schools a little nerve-wracking. I found myself expected to time races (which was all right) and judge diving (which was not), but I survived the term.

I also directed three performances of Molière's *Le Bourgeois Gentilhomme* in which I played M. Jourdain and had the great joy of having Corin Redgrave, a pupil in the Modern Language VI, as a member of the cast. The Director of Music produced the Lully score and we all greatly enjoyed ourselves.

Towards the end of the term I went up to Oxford for the examinations. I really had prepared for them, had read all the books, despite their dreariness, and written my essays. The actual examinations were somewhat farcical. Candidates were leaving after half an hour or so and throughout the whole time. I wrote at some length and used the time to the full. After three days I returned to Westminster for the last few days of what had been a tremendous experience.

The Summer vacation passed quickly and uneventfully. Towards the end of August I received a letter from the Oxford Department of Education. It said: 'We are sorry to inform you that you failed the examination for the Diploma of Education. If you wish to re-take it you will be welcome here in October.' There was no question in my mind of spending another year on 'education' as such. I had already decided that it might be a good idea to improve my academic qualifications and also my spoken French (in those days it was possible to gain a Cambridge degree in Modern Languages without really ever speaking the language) and so I had decided to spend a year in Paris studying for a PhD. I had applied for a post as English assistant in a French Lycée and had been appointed to the Lycée Claude Bernard at the Porte de Saint Cloud in Paris. I had also obtained a room in the Collège Franco-Britannique in the Cité Universitaire. On my way over to France I called in at New College to see some old friends. In the front quad I met the Warden who asked how I had fared in my examinations. I had to admit that I had failed, but hastened to assure him that I had persisted with my work and that the Headmaster of Westminster had told me that he had given me an alpha for my practical teaching assessment. I thought nothing more of it and went on to Paris.

The Collège Franco-Britannique was an extraordinary Victorian style building. The Cité Universitaire has each national building in its own country's style. The Swiss building is a splendid modern building designed by Le Corbusier. I had a room on the second floor and had two French students either side of me, who became close friends for the year. Denis Evesque was studying music and so we shared many interests. Claude Bertrand was a happy-go-lucky student of English who hoped to go into business. We spent many hours in each other's company.

I made my way soon after arrival to the 16th arrondissement.

After the wonderful buildings of Lancing and Westminster, the great modern block of the Lycée Claude Bernard was something of a shock. I met the Headmaster, M. le Directeur, for the first and only time in the year. I was to have only twelve classes a week with a handful of pupils only in each. It was clear that as far as the school was concerned I was something of an unwanted luxury. I met the Head of English and was told to be at the school at 7.55 the next morning. This was something of a shock. At 7.55 there were some 2,000 boys milling around in the central courtyard. At 7.58 a man appeared who blew a whistle. The whole school was immediately silent and the boys formed up into lines. Each line was led – in silence – by a number of men. Some obviously students, others equally obviously retired men to the classroom. The whistle–blower I learnt was M. le Surveillant-Général, the man in charge of school discipline and the line leaders were the 'surveillants', whose sole job in the school was to lead classes to the classrooms, wait until the teacher arrived, then hand over the class and retire to the Common Room or a nearby bar until 5 minutes before the next lesson, at which time they would return to collect the class and escort them in silence to the next classroom. Lessons were from 8.00 a.m. to 12.00 noon, one hour each then an hour's break for lunch and classes from 1.00 p.m.-4.00 p.m. when school closed.

This system of discipline stemmed from Napoleonic times when he had reorganized the whole educational system. It was said even in 1955 that at any time of the day, the Minister of Education could look at his watch and say 'At this moment in every classroom in France all pupils of such and such an age are studying such and such a topic or subject or theory' – another relic of the Napoleonic style. How different it is now. I went back to Claude Bernard on a visit in 1962 and was almost drowned in the flood of humanity that rushed through the corridors between classes with no discipline whatsoever.

There were also a German and an Italian assistant at the Lycée. I think that probably each of the three of us summed up the characteristic that the French expect of their neighbours but we all got on well together. Lunch each day in the staff dining room was always of a high calibre. As I was teaching mainly the older pupils with never more than half a dozen in a class I could take them out of the school – provided that we talked English! As there was a major Rugby football ground and the race course at the Parc de St Cloud in easy walking distance, we could visit those and teaching was indeed a pleasure.

The teaching staff made me very welcome. I had been there about three weeks when in a crowded room one of them said to me in a loud voice: 'There are, you know, only two people in France today who still use the imperfect subjunctive in conversation and they are you and the General (de Gaulle)'. It made me realize, in the ensuing laughter, that I had been extremely well taught but that I needed to relax my efforts with the French language. I was astonished at how many of the pupils committed fundamental errors in their spoken and written French but I soon learned that it was not very tactful and certainly not appreciated when I, 'a foreigner', dared to point out their mistakes to them.

I also obtained an evening post teaching English to assistants from the great Parisian department store 'Le Printemps'. This was quite amusing as they were men and women of all ages who wanted to gain the right to wear a little badge 'Interpreter' for dealing with customers. I was firmly warned by the head of personnel not to get involved socially with any of my pupils as the examiner at the end of the course was – myself – and I could lay myself open to all sorts of bribery! They certainly went out of their way to try to embarrass me. After one lesson a very attractive young girl came to my desk and in broken English said, 'I 'ave been reading an English book, monsieur. It is by a man called Henri Miller.' As I blushed slightly she added, 'I often get feelings like that, monsieur, do you?' Hasty departure of red-faced Englishman.

On another occasion I saw a couple at the back of the class

clearly much involved with each other. I asked the man, in English, 'What are you doing?' In very halting English he replied, 'I am making love'. 'Oh yes' I replied, 'in English or in French?' 'Oh, in French, monsieur.' 'Well, come on out to the front of the class and make it in English'. This managed to calm a potentially chaotic situation.

But it was fun on future visits to Paris to go into the store and seek out former pupils, suitably badged, to see if they had remembered any English and indeed remembered me. Boys at the Lycée Claude Bernard had, on the whole, not been either interested or keen on learning English. The only times I ever managed to arouse any enthusiasm among them was when there was a race meeting at the Saint Cloud racecourse – three minutes walk from the Lycée – when I would take a few of them there and insist that only English was spoken.

One feature of student life in Paris in the 1950s was the fact that one could gain entry to any theatre or concert for a minimum payment. One went to the Box Office half an hour before the show was due to begin and for 100 francs (in those days before devaluation the equivalent of 10p today) could have a seat anywhere that remained in the house. In this way I heard and saw many French works from seats that varied from the orchestra stalls to the upper gallery. I heard many operas that are rarely played outside France – Poulenc's *Les Carmelites*, Lalo's *Le Roi d'Ys*, Charpentier's *Louise* and Massenet's *Thais*, Bizet's *The Pearl Fishers* and Delibes' *Lakmé* among others. There were concerts galore and we were going out four or five times a week.

Memorable among these were concerts given by Gieseking, Rubenstein, Cortot, Furtwängler and a host of French artists. There was one period when over ten days Rubenstein in five concerts performed seventeen piano concertos – and I learned later that he had given the same five concerts during the same ten days in London, flying back and forth across the Channel. Alfred Cortot was the most remarkable of all the artists I heard. He had been accused of collaborating with the Nazis and French orchestras had refused to play with him until one day in 1955 when the Conservatoire orchestra relented. Cortot, then aged 78, played the Schumann Concerto and César Franck Symphonic Variations and then gave encores until midnight. The orchestra had mostly left the platform but the audience remained to a man and he went on until finally he came back once more with coat, hat and gloves on and mimed that he was going to bed. Over a period of some six months I attended many of the Masterclasses he gave on the complete works of Chopin and Schumann, where students would perform for him and he would then comment from time to time, and play the work himself. There would be fistfuls of wrong notes but it has been said of him that they were worth hearing for his musical genius. Certainly the memory of those afternoons is with me still.

There were numerous cafés and cabarets also who would offer students a free place and one free drink provided that one stayed there for a minimum of three hours to give the passing public the impression that the place was pretty full and therefore worth a visit. We spent many evenings in this way also. My colleagues at the Lycée had very kindly put me in touch with various people who wanted private English lessons either for themselves or for their children and had said to these individuals that I had the best English accent in the Lycée and that it would cost 1,000 francs an hour so I had a very useful source of income to supplement the allowance that my father was so generously providing and my modest salary from the French government.

In October, I was very surprised to receive an official letter from the Ministry of Education in England. It read: 'The Minister has reviewed your case and has decided that you should be granted the Diploma of Education.' I had not made any comment about my letter from Oxford which told me that I had failed and so could only conjecture that my chance meeting with Warden Smith in the quadrangle at Oxford had led to some enquiries on his part. Be that as it may, I was thus a qualified teacher! – though it was not a necessary qualification for teaching in an independent school as I hoped to do.

In the meantime I was working on my PhD. I had chosen to write a dissertation on the theatre of Eugène Labiche, whose best known plays are probably *The Italian Straw Hat* and *The Travels of M. Perrichon*, but who wrote over a hundred very amusing comedies and farces. I had read over half of them and was being supervised by a professor at the Sorbonne when in November 1955 I received a letter from the Headmaster of Charterhouse in England. It told me that he was looking for a Modern Linguist to teach mainly Sixth Form French for the academic year beginning September 1956 and that he had heard I might be interested. I was invited back to England for interview, an invitation which I immediately accepted.

I got in touch with my friend John Carleton at Westminster to beg a bed for the night and set off for England a few days later. As I entered Dean's Yard the first person that I met was Walter Hamilton, the Headmaster. 'I hear you are going to teach at Charterhouse', he said. 'Well, I am going there tomorrow for an interview,' I replied. 'Ah yes,' said Walter, 'Brian Young was a boy in my house at Eton and he wrote to ask if I knew of a linguist for him and I said you were not too bad.' So I set off the next morning for Godalming and the interview.

When I was shown in to the very imposing Headmaster's study I must have looked very bemused. A tall, dark and distinguished looking man in full morning dress rose from behind his desk to greet me. 'Don't worry,' he said, 'I don't normally dress like this but I am just off to a wedding.' The interview seemed to go well and in the course of it I found that we had a number of friends in common. He had also been at King's College Cambridge and having acted at the university knew well Donald Beves and Provost Sheppard.

I returned to Paris and four days later to my great joy received a letter offering me the post and telling me that on my return at the end of the academic year I should make contact with the school to see the Head of Department etc. This was a very great excitement which we celebrated (my two French friends and I) with a magnificent dinner at a very expensive Parisian restaurant. As I now had a job lined up I decided to drop work on the PhD and really enjoy Paris and the theatre and music to the full, so for the remainder of the year I indulged in an orgy of theatre and concert going that as I look back on it now seems quite exhausting. It did, however, give me a love of and a knowledge of French music and theatre which I retain to this day.

At the end of the academic year I said goodbye to my two friends, Denis Evesque and Claude Bertrand. We kept in contact for two or three years after but it is now a very long time since I heard from either of them. My year in Paris had made me bilingual and fortunately that fluency with French remains to this day.

Chapter 6

O N MY RETURN to this country, I went down to Charterhouse
and met Roland Le Grand, the Head of Modern Languages. I
learnt also that I was to have rooms in a bachelor colony called
Bernina and after a brief visit went home to South Wales. The
summer holidays passed peacefully with plenty of bowls both at
Barry and Llandrindod. At the start of September I received a letter
from Roland Le Grand enclosing my teaching programme for the
coming year. To my horror I was down to teach German for about
three quarters of the timetable, most of it in the Sixth Form, of
which I knew I was completely incapable. I rushed down to see
him at Charterhouse. 'Oh dear, I forgot that you told me that,' he
declared, 'in that case you have my teaching programme and I will
have yours.' And so I found myself with all the top French
teaching in the school – a daunting prospect but at least not as
horrifically terrifying as that of trying to teach advanced German.

Bernina was a great community. There were seven of us
bachelors there with a 6' 2" housekeeper, Peg Horsfall, who ruled
us all but looked after us magnificently. It was inevitable of course
that the boys would refer to us as Snow White and the Seven
Dwarfs. In fact the previous year they had apparently staged a
Bernina Opera Group performance written by Peter Gardiner, one
of their number, with some co-opted appearances from outside, of
an opera of that name. The doyen of the house was Leonard
Halcrow, a musician and Old Carthusian who had spent most of
his life at Charterhouse apart from being organ scholar at
Peterhouse Cambridge and a disastrous war where he had early on
been captured and spent most of it in a prisoner of war camp. He
was a generous and kind guardian angel for the rest of us.

Brian Young's first words to me were 'All sorts of people will try to involve you in many activities at once but my advice is take a couple of terms to settle in before you commit yourself to anything.' Within six weeks I was co-producing the school play, running the Modern Language Society, helping with the careers advice programme – all of them suggested by Brian Young himself! – and working harder than I ever had in my life with so much Sixth Form work, but loving it. Having coped with the Westminster Modern Language Seventh I found the Charterhouse Sixth pretty straightforward and I was also teaching French throughout the school, with some beginners German, with which I could cope.

My first day in the school as I was walking through, a small man came up to me and said, 'You are Griffiths aren't you? The new Modern Linguist?' 'Yes' I replied cautiously. 'Can you speak French?' 'Yes indeed!' I replied somewhat indignantly, 'I have just lived in Paris for a year. Why do you ask?' 'Last year I was walking past the classroom of the man you are replacing (a man who had twice been Mayor of Godalming) and heard the following. A drone of voices and then a boy saying "Please Sir" "Yes" "Please Sir, that isn't how they say it in France. I know because I live there." "I don't care how they say it in France. This is how we say it at Charterhouse!"' My interlocutor was Wilfred Timms, an outstanding teacher of Spanish and an excellent ex-County Cricketer, who became a very trusted colleague.

The other linguists were Anthony Rowan-Robinson, an elegant Old Wykehamist, Kenneth Chare, an unyielding teacher of German, Wilfred Noyce, an Old Carthusian and a distinguished climber who was sadly killed on a mountain in India some years later and Roland Le Grand himself who, I was soon to find out, as indeed I had already experienced, was one of the nicest but most chaotically disorganized of men.

There was a new language to be learnt. A term is a Quarter and instead of Christmas, Lent and Summer Terms we have Oration,

Long and Cricket Quarters. Work is hash and thus a scholar is a hash-pro. Prep is banco, and so it goes on. The Masters' Common Room, Brooke Hall, is a fine building, more like a gentlemen's club with its large leather armchairs and open fire with club fender before it. There is no central dining hall but each House eats separately. The Housemasters' wives, or housekeeper in the case of a bachelor, deal with the catering individually, which can mean an immense amount of work. We have breakfast and dinner in Bernina but lunch is dependent, unless one is a House Tutor, on invitations to individual Houses. There are dinners in Brooke Hall on Wednesdays and Saturdays for which one may sign in (minimum quorum for a meal is 4). The dinners (3 course) cost 5 shillings a time with unlimited wine for 2 shillings and port at 2 shillings a glass. One signs a chit and receives the bill at the end of the Quarter. The same is true of the help yourself bar in upstairs Brooke Hall. Classes end at 12.45 p.m. each morning and lunch is at 1.30 p.m. which, if not involved with choir practice, cricket practice, play rehearsal or extra teaching, leaves a useful slot for a glass or two of sherry. Brooke Hall is a great institution, but as a young master one soon learns one's place.

About three weeks into my first Quarter, I went into Brooke Hall and seeing a senior colleague sitting in an armchair, bade him good morning. To my astonishment he grunted, stared at me and marched out of the room. Back in Bernina I commented on this. 'Oh we should have warned you. Malaher does not speak to any new member of Brooke Hall for at least two years when he has decided if you are worth speaking to or not!' What was it I had joined?!

At the end of that first Quarter, I read to my horror on the notice board that I was to invigilate Malaher's form in conjunction with him. At least, I thought, he will now have to speak to me. Not a bit of it. A few days later I found four pages of meticulously written instructions for me headed 'Rules in my classroom'. The section that hit home hardest read: 'In my classroom each desk stands on four drawing pins embedded in the floor, and each chair on four more. If, as you walk around every five minutes (the last three words heavily underlined) you can see any of those drawing pins, that boy has been shuffling and idle and will (underlined) be punished.'!! I would spend at least fifteen minutes after each examination session tidying the room and setting desks and chairs in their places.

At the end of the Quarter I received my first pay cheque – for £70! My salary was £450 per annum but £200 was deducted at source for board and lodging and then there was my National Insurance contribution and income tax (minimal). It had been a wonderful thirteen weeks but exhausting and it was clear that it would be some time before I could afford such luxuries as a car or a holiday abroad. I retired back to South Wales for free board and lodging with my long-suffering parents.

On my return in January I was asked if I would like to become a House Tutor. The answer was very definitely yes and so I became the House Tutor of Saunderites with a very remarkable House-master, Eric Harrison, from whom I was to learn so much over the next seven years.

The Headmaster had by tradition been Housemaster of Saunderites but at a common room meeting early in my first Quarter, Brian Young had riveted the assembled company with his opening remarks: 'Gentlemen, I have decided that one of the Housemasters is incompetent and I am going to remove him.' The ten other Housemasters had appropriate reactions to this whilst the younger masters found it highly amusing. Brian Young meant of course that he himself found it very difficult to combine the running of a large school with the running of a large House (72 boys) and Eric succeeded him.

On my first evening on duty I waited in the Housemaster's study for the Head Monitor to collect me to take house prayers. He came in and handed me a book saying: 'I have marked the prayers for you, Sir.' We walked to the dining room where the other 71 members of the House were waiting in a semicircle. The Head Monitor read an extract from the Bible and I then launched into the first prayer. I was halfway through it when I realized that it was a prayer for expectant mothers. Somehow I got through it and told myself that he can't have done it twice – but he had. My other prayer was for schoolmasters who had lost their vocation. As I left the dining room there was a great shout of laughter but I survived and he was an excellent head monitor.

The first year passed swiftly and on the whole peacefully. My education was continuing. One night at dinner in Brooke Hall it was certainly improved. Once the butler had served coffee and port and left the dining room, it was the custom for the youngest member to ask the remaining diners if he could get them anything further. I asked a very senior Housemaster, Bob Arrowsmith, who drank beer at those functions: 'Bob, can I get you another beer?' He was notorious for his very loud voice which now caught the attention of all those dining. 'Young man, no gentleman ever asks another gentleman if he will have another anything. It implies that he has been indulging already. Yes, please, I will have a beer.' So one learns the finer points of life.

During the Summer Holidays my father asked me when I was going to get myself a car. The answer was when I could afford it, which was not for some time yet. On my return to Charterhouse in September, however, the idea caught hold again. Ever since my Lancing days under the influence of Wilfred Derry and Henry Thorold, I had dreamt of owning a Rolls Royce. So early in October Leonard Halcrow and I went up to London to South Kensington to a firm which specialized in old Rolls and Bentleys, to which the owner referred as hes and shes. I finally decided on a 1933 Park Ward 20/25 saloon, a black marvel complete with bulb horn. As I paid over my cheque for £250 I asked the owner if he sold L plates. The look he gave me made me feel that he would withdraw the sale but all was well. Leonard drove the stately machine back to Godalming for me where over the next few months he and Tony Day, another great friend and colleague, taught me to drive.

One of the advantages of being in a school was that I could drive on my own around the roads within the school itself. The boys were much amused by a note in a gossip column of the *Daily Express* 'Seen on a quiet Surrey by-road an otherwise distinguished Rolls Royce bearing L plates. Is this a record?' At any event, six months later I went to Guildford to take my test. I had by this time mastered the art of double de-clutching and manoeuvring backwards despite a minute rear window. Unfortunately though it was raining and the roof leaked over the front passenger seat where the examiner was to sit.

We started off in silence and all went reasonably until we were proceeding down the cobbled Guildford High Street. He warned me that he would give me the signal for an emergency stop. When it came and I slammed on the brakes, the car lurched across the street – a brake drum was clearly worn. Reverse parking left the car about 18 inches from the kerb and by now the examiner was pretty wet. I drove back to the driving centre anticipating a failure. 'Well, Mr Griffiths, you can go back and face your pupils. You have passed.' I thanked him and apologized for the soaking he had undergone. 'No matter. Could I have a look at the engine? I have got a 1935 Park Ward myself.' And so in the pouring rain we pored over the engine. I had been lucky once again in finding an examiner who was also a vintage car enthusiast.

In Summer 1957 we had a visit from Her Majesty the Queen and HRH Prince Philip Duke of Edinburgh. I was helping one of the Housemasters, Tony White, with his production of *Henry VI part I* by William Shakespeare. My most difficult task was trying to keep 16 boys in full armour quiet while waiting in the wings for their entry on stage. The visit was a great success and Prince Philip came to watch part of a rehearsal. Because of his predilection for science he had spent more time than expected in the Science Laboratories and so his visit to the rehearsal (which had been repeated three or four times before he appeared!) was a brief one but nevertheless much appreciated. The royal party had arrived by helicopter which landed on the Cricket Field – not on the Cricket Square, it was carefully pointed out – and the Queen duly asked for, and was given, an extra half-holiday in honour of the visit.

During the Summer Term, sorry, Cricket Quarter, I received a splendid invitation. One of my fellow Bernina inmates, Peter Gardiner, was a keen opera fan and he and I had made several visits to Covent Garden. We had also spent the half-term weekend in a hotel near Glyndebourne which had enabled us to have two memorable visits to that opera house. Now Peter asked me what were my plans for the Summer Holidays. It turned out that his parents had been planning to take him to Salzburg to the music festival but on their arrival back in England (Peter's father, an ex-military man, was now in charge of the railway system of a South American country) Mrs Gardiner had been diagnosed with mild TB and was in a sanatorium in Sussex. The invitation was for me to take her place in the visit to Salzburg.

It was a wonderful experience. The Brigadier drove us, and each evening at bedtime we were issued with the orders for the following day. Breakfast 0730 hours, departure 0815 hours and so on in a very military style. We arrived safely in Salzburg and for a week had an orgy of concert and opera going. The operas we heard were *The Marriage of Figaro* (with a dream star-studded cast), *Die Entführung aus dem Serail* and in the open air Felsenreitschule, Richard Strauss's *Elektra* conducted by Dimitri Mitropoulos. There were morning and afternoon chamber concerts and evening orchestral concerts (when we were not at the opera). The week passed all too quickly and we returned to England for another summer of bowls.

On my return to Charterhouse in January 1958 I found that Roland Le Grand was ill and there was no replacement for him. For the next ten weeks I was teaching Sixth Form classes of 32 pupils as Roland's and my sets were combined. With essays, proses

and unseens to correct it was the hardest I had ever worked in my
life but great fun. About a week after returning for the Cricket
Quarter (after a short Easter Holiday which passed too quickly in
an exhausted heap) I awoke one morning to find that my face
seemed to have become lopsided. On coming downstairs to
breakfast my bachelor colleagues decided unanimously that I had
lockjaw 'as a result of talking so much!' I could not keep food in
my mouth and in a panic rushed to the school Sanatorium to see
the school doctor, Joe Waycott. After one look at me he said, 'Oh
good, I've always wanted to study someone with this. You have
Bell's Palsy, but if you do as I say you will be all right within six
months.' This was not very encouraging news. It meant that I took
up residence in the Sanatorium for the whole of that Summer
Term. At first, I could not close my left eye and had to wear an eye
patch; also I could not really manage to eat and for about 10 days
was on liquids only through a straw. Joe would come in several
times a day to stick needles in parts of my face to measure how the
illness was progressing.

My main worry was my Sixth Form teaching with A levels in
about six weeks' time. My bed was put in one of the larger wards
and my Sixth formers came in and lay on the various beds in the
room in a manner rather reminiscent of the old Roman teachers
and their pupils, whilst I attempted – pretty unsuccessfully – to
speak French with no control over my jaw and lip movements. But
we got through the work and the memory of those sessions
remained with the boys for many years to come, as I was
frequently reminded by them at Old Boy gatherings over the next
years. After about a month I could dispense with the eye patch and
gradually my mouth became more easily manoeuvrable. Just across
the road from the Sanatorium was a large house which had been
built at the turn of the century by a retired Housemaster. When Dr
Haig Brown had brought the school down from London in 1872
the individual Housemasters were expected to run their Houses on
their own financially. It would seem that some of them had not fed

their pupils too lavishly and had amassed reasonable fortunes as there were several large houses around the school built by retired housemasters from that era. The one in question was now owned by St Thomas' Hospital in London and was used as a training college for new nurses. The two sisters in charge, Catherine Gamelin and Jane Davies learnt that there was a case of Bell's Palsy readily to hand and for the next few weeks I was exhibited to countless groups of young nurses, which certainly increased my reputation amongst the senior boys of Charterhouse. It had the great advantage of gaining me friendship with two very remarkable ladies, which lasted for many years and meant several very enjoyable visits to parties in London at St Thomas'.

An interesting sidelight on my illness was that I had persuaded my younger brother Richard, by then studying at King's Cambridge for his PhD, to come down to Charterhouse to take my lower classes – I kept the Sixth Form for myself! I was fortunate in that I taught the top set at O level and the scholars in their first year apart from the Sixth Form, and also an O level German set. Richard, with a First Class degree in his BA examinations and a very scholarly approach to language, seemed to me a far more than adequate substitute for myself. It is very interesting how teaching varies at different levels. After about three weeks he came to see me in the San. almost in tears. 'They are so stupid – they don't seem able to understand what I am saying.' I then learnt that in the scholars' class, when he had said 'Stop talking' for the 50th time in one lesson, the whole class had cheered and stood on their desks. With permission from Joe Waycott I made my way to my classroom and read the riot act and I am glad to say that Richard did not have any further disciplinary problems but it was not an experience that he enjoyed or would ever repeat in his career.

By the end of term, Joe Waycott pronounced me reasonably cured and so I went back to South Wales for a Summer Holiday of relaxation.

In September 1958 I was able to return to Charterhouse fairly nearly fully recovered. My face would still, when I was tired, betray that I had had something wrong but over the years it has gradually become fully restored. I was fortunate indeed that I had had a doctor who knew what was required and a Headmaster who was prepared to let me be somewhat of a passenger for a whole term. And that is to say nothing of a Sanatorium Sister of the old school, Mollie Gilbert, who looked after me wonderfully but kept firm discipline in her San. When she found out that a couple of my Bernina allies had smuggled in a bottle of gin and some tonics for me they – and I – were made to feel like naughty small boys!

Back in school meant a return to my classroom in C block, one of the oldest parts of Charterhouse, where my classes and I had to walk through another master's classroom to get in to mine. This colleague was one of the most eccentric characters I have ever met in my life. A.R.B. Fuller, known to the boys as Fats Fuller after the great jazz musician Fats Waller, had been set for Cambridge when his father became bankrupt. To earn the money to get himself to the University he got a job in London as a bank runner and thus became very interested in the City and its customs. He became a member of the Fishmongers' and the Wax Chandlers' Companies and when I met him was also Librarian at St Paul's Cathedral. He lived in Barnet, North London, and cared for his elderly mother. Each day he would be up at 5.30 a.m. to wash and feed her, would then catch the first Tube train from Barnet at 6.30 a.m. to Waterloo, train to Godalming and a quick walk up the hill to the school, arriving in time for first lesson at 9.00 a.m. He would go back each day after afternoon lessons arriving at Barnet in time to get his mother's supper and settle her for the night. This he had been doing for some 17 years when I met him and he continued to follow this routine 6 days a week until he retired from teaching in 1967. He always claimed that the train was the warmest place in which to do his corrections! On half-holidays, he would leave after lunch and spend the afternoon in the Library at St Paul's before going home. (A neighbour looked after the old lady at lunchtime.) Fats' knowledge of the public schools and also of senior church figures was encyclopaedic. He taught the bottom form in the school and had them for all subjects except French, maths and the sciences. He had very poor discipline and his classroom was pretty chaotic. At the end of each day he would ask me to help him clear it up – resulting in two wastepaper baskets full of sweet wrappings, tins, sandwich papers, paper darts etc. One day, one of the cleaners stopped me to comment on how tidy Mr Fuller's room always was! One desk was in pristine condition (whereas the others were heavily engraved) and no-one was allowed to use it. It was 'reserved for Prince Charles' who, of course, did not attend Charterhouse in his career.

If he wished to leave his class early, he would burst into my classroom, whoever I might be teaching, would genuflect and intone the words: 'Lead me not into temptasion'; to which I would reply: 'But deliver us from evil' – this meant 'I am off to London'; 'I will look after your classroom for you' – and off he would go. The boys got used to this performance but a young student master who was observing me teach on one occasion was much mystified. Brian Young, the Headmaster, who occasionally taught in Fats' room said to me one day: 'I have to be away tomorrow at a meeting but I understand that you and Fuller have an arrangement, so will you keep an eye on my class in the afternoon?' – we did not have the same ecclesiastical verbal exchange!

In one classroom there was a plaque on the wall which read '. . . . . . taught and inspired in this classroom for 30 years.' When Fuller retired, it was suggested by some of his younger colleagues that we should subscribe for a plaque for his classroom with the words: 'ARB Fuller fought and perspired in this classroom for 22 years,' but sadly it never came to fruition.

I had been at Charterhouse for 6 years when Fuller said to me one day: 'Do you intend to remain a schoolmaster?' I assured him that I did, so he continued: 'In that case, you really should have one serious outside interest. Would you care to become a Wax Chandler?' I knew nothing whatsoever about the City of London or the Livery Companies but said yes and so a few years later was admitted as a Freeman of that Company and in 1990, in fact, became Master of it, of which I shall tell more later. Fuller was the Master when he invited me to join and was, I found out later, engaged in a recruiting campaign, but thanks to him, I was introduced to something that has given, and indeed continues to give, me great pleasure and satisfaction.

I mentioned earlier that I had been invited to co-produce the school play. It was *Henry IV part I* and my most difficult task was trying to usher 15 or so boys in full armour in silence up the wooden stairs which led from under the stage into the wings of the dais in the Great Hall, which was at that time used for all dramatic productions. It was virtually impossible! One of the cast, a page-boy, was Nicky Henson, son of the great Leslie, so for the second time in my career I had a future star of the stage in a production of mine. Brooke Hall put on a play every year which was always a surefire success with the school. I had the good fortune to play Algernon in *The Importance of Being Earnest*, and Charles in *Blithe Spirit*. In the latter play I borrowed from a boy in my house an extremely exotic dressing gown very much in the Noel Coward style. At the post play party, one of the guests commented on it and wondered whether I realized that the designs on it were, in fact, fertility symbols, at which point both the ladies playing my two wives collapsed with laughter and confessed to all present that they were both pregnant – not I hasten to say anything to do with me or the play! We also put on *Ten Sixty Six and All That*, the book of which had, of course, been written by W.E. Sellar who had been a Housemaster at Charterhouse. His widow, Hope, took part in the performance as one of Henry VIII's wives and told us that Walter used to wake her up at 3.00 a.m. to try out his latest witty saying for the book – if she laughed at that time of day it was in. Another play was *Dick Whittington Comes to Charterhouse* – written by Peter

A rehearsal of Henry IV part I at Charterhouse; Duke of Edinburgh (seated); standing (l. to r.) Brian Young, Headmaster, Tony White and author.

Gardiner and in which I played Lord Battersea South, a Conservative peer in a duet with Lord Battersea North, a Labour peer.

I also translated Jules Romain's play *Le Docteur Knock* into English and we had a hilarious time in rehearsals and performances. This really is one of the great farces of all time, and once again *Le Bourgeous Gentilhomme* in French with the Modern Language VI. I was the much padded M. Jourdain and my wife was played by Alastair Sawday, who nowadays has made a name for himself as the author of numerous books describing hotels and B&Bs in France and other European countries.

In the meantime in 1958 I was elected as Secretary of Brooke Hall in succession to Leonard Halcrow. It was a wonderful position to have. I was responsible for the twice weekly dinner (including the seating plans if there were a number of guests) and for the wine cellar, which carried a large number of wines. I found that at the outbreak of the Second World War there had been a full Common Room meeting to discuss what to do with the reserve funds they held. The choice was War Loan or Vintage port and in 1959 we were drinking the 1927 port which had been laid down in the cellars under the main buildings, having been purchased at five shillings a bottle. I was selling it at two shillings a glass at the twice weekly dinners! The vote had been unanimous! I had a staff of four, butler Wickens and members of his family to cook and serve, with more available if we had a large number of people dining. All events that took place in Brooke Hall, including entertainment of visiting staff on match days, were my responsibility and in the summer holidays, the Old Boys' Cricket XI, the Charterhouse Friars, took it over for their cricket week. One of my tasks was to deliver wine, beer and spirits orders to Housemasters on a weekly basis for which the old Rolls Royce came in very useful. It was good also to have a car large enough to contain the school fives team, if there was an away match and so I arranged to visit a number of other establishments in this way.

In the Summer Holidays I had my first real triumph at Llandrindod Wells. I had reached the last eight or the last four in various competitions there in previous years but now I found myself in the first week in the final of the Ormathwaite Cup. En route to the final I had managed to beat Percy Watson, Captain of the current Irish Bowling Team and two current Welsh internationals and one Scottish international (the competition was pretty hot in those days). My opponent in the final was Arthur Knowling, from Worthing, the current Captain of the English Team. I was told before the game that he had been playing in competitive bowls the whole season (beginning in mid-April and it was now mid-August) and had only lost two matches in that time. After an hour, I was losing 8-17, which meant that on any end if he scored a full house of 4 shots I had lost. After two hours, the score was 20-20 and I had one bowl left. I needed, over a distance of some 30 yards, to touch one of my own bowls from a horizontal to a vertical position. If I moved it over completely, it would push the jack nearer to Arthur's bowl, which was holding shot. If I missed, he had won. This is where the element of luck I referred to earlier came in. I delivered the bowl – it was near its target! Then I saw Arthur running up the green towards me to congratulate me – I had won my first tournament! I looked at my father who had been at the greenside throughout. He had smoked a whole packet of cigarettes in the excitement of the moment. As a result of this I was to play in the Welsh under 35 side against England under 35s the following month.

I was also bowling in Surrey and was listed in the programme as Roger Griffiths, Weybridge BC, but everyone knew my father and I was, and still am, a Welshman!

Back at Charterhouse, work continued as ever. I was still learning so much about the art of schoolmastering from Eric Harrison and I was still enjoying myself very much but in the course of that term it was suggested that I might like to consider an exchange of a year with a master from the USA. I went up to

London to the English Speaking Union for an interview and learnt a couple of weeks later that I had been given a Fulbright Exchange Scholarship. In the course of the next few months, I learnt that my exchangee was to be a certain Dick Flood from an independent boys boarding school in Connecticut called Pomfret. I knew only that he was married with a son of four and a baby son of a few weeks, so I had to find a house for them for the year – they would not have fitted in to bachelor Bernina! This I succeeded in doing and so at the beginning of September I went to Southampton to board the *Queen Mary* with 107 other exchange teachers.

Chapter 7

A s I walked up the gangway on board the *Queen Mary* in Southampton with many other passengers, I noticed that down below me there was a stream of men disembarking from the lower deck. Shortly after we learnt that they had been the crew and that there was a strike under way. For 48 hours we remained tied up at the quayside. The *Queen Mary* was a beautiful ship built in the style of a really luxurious 1930s hotel with wood panelling and high ceilings in all the main rooms. I was to share my cabin with another exchange schoolmaster and for those 48 hours we savoured and enjoyed to the full the delights of the ship. Then came the announcement that the exchange party were to re-pack their luggage, taking with them only 44 lbs in weight as we were to be flown from Heathrow to New York. Our remaining belongings would catch up with us some seven weeks later! There were 104 of us in the group.

During our brief stay on the *Queen Mary* we had been given a briefing on what we might expect in the USA. I remember particularly that we were told that we should never say if we strongly disliked something about the country as that would not endear us to our hosts. We should declare 'How very interesting' with no further comment. We were also warned not to walk alone in Central Park New York even in the daytime and never to give lifts to hitchhikers as there were people (and lawyers) who made a living from this by asking to be set down somewhere and then 'accidentally' (though maintaining that it was the fault of the driver) falling out of the vehicle before it actually stopped.

I had never flown in my life. The thought alone terrified me and though I could readily believe that more harm was likely to occur to me when crossing the road in our village, it nevertheless filled me with a deep sense of worry. But there was no turning back. As we boarded the 747 I caused a certain amount of amusement to my fellow travellers by asking the stewardess where my parachute was and there followed eight hours of misery. We arrived in New York to find a temperature of 90 degrees (it had been 50 in England when we left) with a 95% humidity and to add to the discomfort there was a strike of baggage handlers and the 85 ladies in our group felt too overwhelmed by the heat to carry their luggage so the 19 men had to work extra hard.

We had four days of briefing preparation for the year together with a little sightseeing. One evening I was with another male exchange teacher at the bar in our hotel when we started chatting to an American there. He was aged about 60 and in New York on his own. He invited us to have dinner with him that evening 'as he was lonely on his own' and took us to an amazing restaurant where I had the largest steak I had ever seen and eaten in my life. It completely overlapped the whole large dinner plate and was simply delicious. We found out later that this was the speciality of that restaurant and our kind Texan friend had wanted to show the Limeys what his state could produce. We went back to the hotel full to the gills and aware once again of the generosity of so many Americans. When our briefing ended I went down to the docks to meet briefly my exchange, Dick Flood and his wife and family, and see them off on the ship, the *United States*, which I found very chromium plated and unattractive compared with the *Queen Mary*. Dick had driven his large Chevrolet estate car, or station wagon as I learnt to call it, to the docks and it was for me to take over and drive to Cape Cod to meet up with his family for a welcoming party. I was relieved that I had learnt to drive on a large vehicle as this car was, or seemed to be, enormous. Also it was a left-hand drive and though I had driven on the continent and therefore on the right hand side of the road, it had always been in a right-hand drive car. I ventured cautiously into the streets of New York and finally saw the number of the Thruway Dick had told me to take. It was about 4.30 p.m. and the traffic was intense. It is a twelve-lane highway and in the evening rush hour 10 lanes are going out of the city and 2 coming in and the reverse in the mornings. I drove along in about lane 5 at the speed everyone else was taking (roughly 55 mph). After about an hour I saw a sign indicating a turn off but with no mention of where I wanted to go. Some 30 minutes later I realized that I was heading north when I should have been going south! It took me nearly another hour to move from lane 5 to the inside lane in order to exit.

I telephoned the Flood family and explained my error. They were very kind and said the party had started but they looked forward to meeting me in due course! By the time I found their house it was 10.30 p.m. and the party had broken up. I had a brief snack and was then shown my room and slept soundly until the next morning.

The Floods senior were the most delightful couple. He had been for some years Deputy Head of a private school in Boston called Noble and Greenough School where I was to spend many happy days in the course of my year. For the time being though we were to go up to Maine to their holiday home – and we drove there the next day. It was a wonderful experience driving up through the whole of New England. I had heard of the Fall colours and they were breathtaking. I went wild with my camera and took far too many wonderful photographs. In Maine, the cottage was in a small settlement called Blue Hill where we spent two weeks. One joy was to go down in the early evening to the small harbour to buy lobsters from the boats as they came in, which we cooked and ate on the beach straight after. The main event of the year was the Blue Hill Fair – a real taste of the early American countryside with the modern addition of a quite startling sideshow called 'The Streets of Paris' which Dick's younger brother and I visited – much to the disgust of the Floods senior!

And then it was time to make my way to Pomfret School in

Connecticut. Like so many of the New England independent schools it was built in neo-Georgian style with a great lawn in front of the main buildings and a small stone Chapel beside it. I presented myself at the school office when in swept a man of about 50 in casual gear who introduced himself to me as Dave Twichell, the Headmaster. His exceptionally casual approach was to be a feature of the year and yet it worked remarkably well.

I was to be in charge of the ground floor of one of the dormitory blocks with about 20 senior boys in individual study bedrooms and my own apartment – a very spacious sitting room, small bedroom, bathroom and kitchen. The first thing I did was to switch off the central heating which seemed to me very excessive. Several weeks into the term when boys had been constantly complaining of the cold (something I had not noticed) one of them pointed out to me that the control in my apartment was a control for the whole floor of the building and so I spent the rest of the autumn and winter in a cocoon of warmth! Within a few hours of my settling in, my colleague who was in charge of the upper floor, came in to introduce himself. Pete Marble, who was head of English studies and Director of Drama, was a real character.

His opening remark was to suggest that I went with him to the Pomfret Village Store to lay in supplies for the winter. 'Just buy the same as I do' was his advice. To my astonishment this was 2 one-gallon jars of gin, a gallon of Bourbon whisky, a gallon of sherry, 36 cans of beer and a good supply of tonics. I soon realized that Pete had a serious drink problem and early on gave up any attempt to go drink for drink with him. He was a generous dispenser of drinks but he (and I of course) had finished what I had taken to be a six months' supply within my first month in the school. He could certainly hold his liquor though the boys on his floor had many occasions I fear when they had to put him to bed. He was a very skilled producer of plays and memorable during the year were performances of *Guys and Dolls* and *West Side Story*.

The Head of Languages was Marcel Marcotte, a most engaging

French Canadian who very generously gave me a good slice of his Sixth Form French teaching. To my astonishment I found that the American boys were about two years behind their opposite numbers in the UK. The standard of work was therefore a great relaxation for me but I managed to arouse some enthusiasm. During the year we did in fact stage my old favourite, Molière's *Le Bourgeois Gentilhomme*, with the Lully music which was a great innovation for the school – but French with very strong American accents was always a worry for me. German was run by Marga König who gave me some beginners' German classes to work with but I only had 24 classes a week (compared with 33 at Charterhouse) so that my life was relatively easy. Marga appeared very stern and strict when one met her but she was, in fact, a kind and helpful soul who was appreciated by her pupils and colleagues.

I became great friends with another of the French teachers, Russell Stringer, whose nickname to the boys was 'Le Baron'. His apartment was filled with the most elaborate French furniture, abounding in gold and gilt decorations. He was a great character, elegantly dressed and always with the hint of aristocratic French background and ancestors. I was to have many good evenings and a splendid holiday to Florida with Russ.

My greatest friends, as they are to this day, were George and Maggie Bartlett and their two children, Polly, then aged about 4 and Peter, about 18 months. George's father was headmaster of South Kent School, which I was to visit later in the year. George taught history and was much involved with sport, particularly rowing. As a family they were kindness itself to me – but so were most members of the faculty. Pomfret was a small school but a very happy and united common room. It was interesting that out of a group of twenty masters, six were to go on to become Headmasters, which later in my career gave me useful contacts for pupil exchanges and visits.

I had a few days to settle in and then came the first day of term, beginning as in England with a staff meeting. In came Dave

Twichell with the opening greeting: 'Gee, gang, great to have you back here and we're going to have a wow of a year'. On my return to Charterhouse I told Brian Young of his American opposite number's start to the year and he began the Charterhouse Common Room meeting as follows: 'Roger Griffiths tells me that my American counterpart began the school year with the words "gee, gang great to have you back and we're going to have a wow of a year" and though I might express myself somewhat differently, my feelings are precisely those of my American counterpart.' The meeting was not long at Pomfret. I was welcomed officially into the school and there were a few notices and it was time for lunch.

The boys arrived back and I met the families who were entrusting their sons to my care for twelve months. The most startling thing to me was the boys' appearance. I had already grown used to the American informality of dress and behaviour – but here were young men in blazers with school crest, grey flannels, white shirts and school ties, with short haircuts and impeccable manners. 1960 was still the heyday of the formality à l'anglaise of the American independent schools – when I returned on a visit in 1972 it had all changed and informality of dress, appearance and manners were the order of the day, and co-education! As it was in 1960 I felt very much at home.

I soon got used to the routine. A bell went at 6.00 a.m., breakfast in the school dining hall was at 7.00 a.m., then back to my apartment, inspect the boys' rooms at 7.45 a.m. and classes at 8.00 a.m. until 12.00 noon; a half hour break and lunch at 12.30 p.m., games to watch and try to understand (baseball, field hockey, soccer and fencing – then later in the winter, ice hockey and rowing and baseball or tennis and swimming in the summer). Classes from 4.00 p.m. to 6.00 p.m., supper at 6.30 p.m. for the boys and then quiet in the buildings as they did their prep until 9.00 p.m. Lights out at 10.30 p.m. It was not so different from England and yet it was. Most evenings I would either cook myself a meal or would get together with Russ or Pete Marble for a meal.

The married faculty members were immensely generous in entertaining us. It was a source of amusement to them that if invited out I would walk across the campus to their homes – 200-300 yards – rather that take the car as they would!

In the dining hall there were tables for 10 people and each faculty member had a table – in my case with 9 boys who moved around in rotation from table to table every two weeks. Married faculty had their family with them – even the very small – which could mean fewer boys at certain tables. The food was of a good standard and there was plenty of it so that grumbles were rare. It was an excellent way of getting to know the whole school for there were about 200 pupils altogether and thus one met them all during the year. The conviviality of Brooke Hall seemed far away but the friendliness of everyone at Pomfret made up for it.

Towards the end of November there was great excitement in the school. It was the Dance weekend, when girl friends could come to visit for the weekend, staying in one dormitory block which had been cleared of boys. At school assembly before it began, Dave Twichell reminded the school of no alcohol and no smoking rules. The girls arrived and watched a football match and then – everyone was summoned to the school hall by the Headmaster. 'An empty beer can has been found outside the buildings – I insist that whoever put it there owns up or the weekend is cancelled.' Silence for two full minutes and general consternation setting in. Then a small female voice near to tears: 'Gee Mr Twichell, I reckon it must have been me. I used a can of beer to wash my hair because it gives it a sparkle!' General relief and the weekend passed without a hitch though it was difficult on Monday morning to get the boys' concentration back on to French irregular verbs.

Towards the end of term there was a Carol service in the Chapel which reminded me so much of England, and then it was holiday time. I was to have five days in New York before going out to Cape Cod to join the Bartlett family for Christmas. I stayed in New York at the Harvard Club of New York thanks to a reciprocal arrangement my club in London, the Oxford and Cambridge, had with them. It was a building and atmosphere reminiscent indeed of a London club but I was there for bed and breakfast only. I went to the Metropolitan Opera House for *La Bohème*, the *Marriage of Figaro* and *Tannhauser*, each with casts from the gramophone catalogues, one concert at Carnegie Hall and then *West Side Story*, *Rose*, with Ethel Merman as Gypsy Rose Lee and finally on only the fifth night of its opening run in New York, *Camelot* with Richard Burton and Julie Andrews. Friends at Pomfret had told me that that was one show I would not get to as it was sold out for nine months ahead but ever optimistic I queued and found a single returned seat for that evening. It was magnificent and rounded off an unbelievable visit to the Big Apple. I had also managed to do all the usual sightseeing – Empire State Building, Statue of Liberty and the Cathedral – and so a gentle rest on Cape Cod was needed.

Christmas chez Bartlett was a joy. Sam Bartlett, George's father, was an amazing man who had spent his whole life, man and boy at South Kent School and was now near retiring but still in full spate. In appearance he was an American Norman Wisdom and he had a wonderful New England dry wit. Thanks to him I ate, and disliked intensely, my first oysters but I found him and his dear wife excellent company and George and Maggie's hospitality was boundless. On Christmas morning we all went to church and then walked on the beach where snow lay on the sand under a cloudless blue sky. Altogether a memorable day. I telephoned home and spoke at length with my parents and brother.

After a few more happy days it was back to Pomfret which was still under snow. It had snowed from the end of October and would continue from time to time until April. However, by 6.30 each morning a path would have been cleared from the door of my apartment to the dining hall and by 8.00 a.m. all school roads were clear. In Connecticut they send snowploughs out at the slightest hint of snow and so one was able to drive safely throughout that whole winter. The Lent Term passed by without great incident apart from the fact that I fell ill and was diagnosed with alcohol poisoning – too much trying to keep up with Marble. The Easter holidays were devoted to a holiday with Russ Stringer. We drove south in his car to Washington for a couple of days sightseeing then on to Charleston (two more days of sightseeing) and then on to Miami which even in April was warm and sunny. Miami was unbelievable. The hotels were on the grandest scale with, for example, statues of the Venus de Milo and the Winged Victory (though twice the size of the originals) outside the main entrance. Russ decided to show me the inside of one hotel and was infuriated to be refused entry by the doorman as 'we were not wearing ties', which seemed splendidly olde-worldly. The extra large elderly and middle-aged ladies in mink bikinis with diamond studded sun glasses were a bit hard to take but a visit to the Florida Glades and an alligator ranch brought us back to reality. We drove out over the Florida Keys to Key West, an amazing road hopping from key to key over the ocean, and in general it had been a memorable holiday.

Back at school it dawned on me that my year was rushing past. I spent part of the term visiting as many schools in New England as I could. There were some five establishments, notably Groton, Phillips Andover and Phillips Exeter, where friends of the Floods taught and where I was made most welcome. The most astonishing visit was to Deerefield School, Pete Marble's old school, where the Headmaster, Frank Boyden, had been Head for over 50 years. He kept his desk in the hall in the main entrance to the school so that he could personally see every one who came into or went out of the establishment. The day we arrived there his desk was covered in photographs. These were of the boys coming to join the school that autumn and he was learning them so that he could greet each one by name on his arrival. He was then in his 83rd year and his wife, aged 80 and totally blind, was the head of science and still teaching amazingly well. He insisted on 100% devotion from his staff to the school in term time and then they could have complete run of all the many facilities for themselves, family and friends throughout the holidays. He was certainly a one-off as headmasters go. A highlight of the Summer Term was a production of Gilbert and Sullivan's *Patience*, which I produced with staff and wives involved. We slightly re-wrote the operetta. The Grenadier Guards became the Pomfret Football Team, Patience was a waitress at a drive-in snack bar, Bunthorne and Grosvenor were lower New York beatnik poets, the Colonel was the football coach etc. Somehow it worked – the school orchestra performed nobly and the American accents coped with G&S lyrics. I, as Bunthorne, remained the one English voice in the production but the school, and their parents, loved it. Warren Geissinger, the Director of Music, was still talking of it on his last visit to the UK in 1990.

About halfway through the Summer Term a parent came to see me and asked if I would spend a month of the Summer Holidays driving his son and two schoolfriends around the United States – car and all petrol provided and a credit card to pay for all meals and hotels. It was a wonderful opportunity and I jumped at it. In the event at the very last moment I contracted glandular fever and had to forego the trip, which was very disappointing.

The school was about to close and I was ill in bed in my apartment. Then help arrived in the shape of a very good friend of Russ Stringer's, Freda Polk, who lived near the school and insisted that I went to recuperate at her house. She was kindness itself and within two to three weeks I was feeling much better. Then Pete Marble stepped in and said that he would take me with him on a tour up north into Canada. We set off in his car, with appropriate refreshment in the boot. We drove up through New Hampshire and Maine and reached the Canadian border. As we crossed into Canada Pete suddenly realized that the Gaspé peninsula, which we were to explore, was dry! We filled the car up at a nearby liquor store and set off. The Gaspé peninsula is quite striking as a scenic route but the poverty of many of the inhabitants was horrific. As we drove through villages it was quite common for a child to rush in front of the car. As we braked violently to a halt the car would be surrounded by all the members of the family carrying carved model ships or lace clothes which they had made and hoped to sell to the tourists. We learnt that they train their children to run in front of cars for this purpose and if one is occasionally killed – well the family is too large anyway! It was a horrific way of life with which to be confronted.

We had two weeks of travel and then returned to Pomfret where I had a round of farewell parties with invitations to many colleagues to come over to England and I then left the Flood car at school and went by train to New York to catch the *Queen Elizabeth I* back to England. It was a fine ship and the five days passed too quickly.

What would I remember of the United States? Firstly the warmth and friendliness of the people I had met. I think one should never judge a country by the inhabitants who leave it as tourists. There have been many times in my life when travelling in France or Germany I have been acutely embarrassed by the behaviour of compatriots who are also visiting those countries. I think that the same is often true of many Americans who visit Europe. They are not typical of the American race who, as I found, can be quiet and undemanding and unassuming, but above all friendly and welcoming. Then there is the vastness of the country and the diversity of it. I had in the course of my year visited most of the East Coast of the USA – and it was on later visits that I went West but even on the East Coast there is such variety from rural Maine through urban splendour in New York and Washington to elegant surroundings in Charleston and Carolina to vulgar ostentation in Miami and amazing beauty on the Keys. Of American education I think the memory is of ordinariness. They are interested in their own history and geography and literature but not so much of the rest of the world. They are insistent on high grades even from work, much of which is mediocre in standard. I think that over the past 40 years this situation had improved considerably – that was my feeling at the time.

But my abiding memory was of a happy year where I had learnt much, had made many new friends and had acquired an independence of outlook which had been lacking before.

I returned home for three weeks to South Wales before the Oration Quarter 1961 at Charterhouse.

Living in my own apartment at Pomfret had given me a taste for being on my own at Charterhouse. I informed Bernina that I intended to do this. Only Leonard Halcrow was upset as he felt it was a rejection of the camaraderie there but he got over that. I had a set of rooms with my own kitchenette in a house near the school belonging to a pleasant couple called Dick and Drena Dewar. It was good to be back on full-time teaching but there was a shock in store for me. Dick and Sally Flood had been much liked at Charterhouse and had had a most successful year but unfortunately Dick's teaching was not at the same level as mine. To be fair to him, he had never been to France, the only French literature he had read was in translation and he had no German. He had been offered professional contracts as a baseball player and American football player and was a very competent ice hockey player but language teaching was not his forte! (You may well wonder how the ESU had planned the exchange of two such different people but amazingly it had worked for each of us.) It meant, however, that all my senior teaching had been taken over by the other linguists who had enjoyed it so that on my return I found I was only teaching lower sets and only up to O level standard. However, before too long my Sixth Form was restored to me.

Chapter 8

IN THE YEAR BEFORE I had left for Connecticut I had sold my
1933 Rolls and bought for £100 a green 1927 Rolls 25-30. It was
a stately machine, top speed 40 mph but my mother had been
worried by it and persuaded my father to give me his Rover 75
provided that I disposed of the Rolls. The Rover was in fact
heavier on the steering than the Rolls had been. During my year
away I had lent it to Antony Rowan-Robinson, who on my return
gave me a magnificent eighteenth-century wing armchair in
which I sit now as I write this, as a thank you. But I missed the
Rolls. My brother had just passed his driving test and my father
had offered to buy him a car so I achieved the rather dubious
success of selling back to my father a car which he had given me!
Richard took over the Rover and I found a magnificent 1936 Rolls
which could manage a reasonable speed and was a joy to drive. It
cost £300 and was certainly worth it. Wilfred Derry from Lancing
had introduced me to a friend of his, Shane Chichester, who had
been chief salesman with Rolls Royce. In 1914 he had driven the
lead Rolls, a magnificent white 40/50, of the team of six Rolls sent
out to France for the C-in-C of the army. Now in retirement he
lived near Charterhouse with his wife and a collection of six
vintage Rolls Royce. His gardener had been a chief mechanic with
the firm – when any Rolls belonging to a friend needed a service
Shane would undertake this with his gardener and would lend the
friend a vehicle from his collection for the week or so that the
service took. I was thus enabled to produce a variety of
magnificent cars over the years, which raised my stock with the
pupils of Charterhouse. In the Cricket Quarter of 1962 the Rolls
Royce Club of Great Britain held a rally in the grounds of

Charterhouse, which was a great spectacle for pupils and visitors alike.

In the Summer Holidays, Tony Day, Dick Crawford and I went on a trip to France in the Rolls. We were down on the Loire in the village of Langeais and went to several Son et Lumière spectacles in the area. On our return northwards we stopped in Saint Denis to visit the Basilica. Unfortunately, the Rolls had developed the unfortunate habit of back-firing loudly when I switched off the engine. On this occasion we were parked outside the local Gendarmerie. It was at a time when there had been problems with Algerian terrorists and at the sound of the explosion from the car, three gendarmes immediately rushed out with machine guns at the ready. It took an explanation in my very best, and most grovelling, French to calm them down and satisfy them – but we got back to England safely.

At Charterhouse I had now moved to a house in Mark Way, just across the main road from the school. It was owned by Kit and Yole Wilson, a cousin of my colleague Bob Arrowsmith, and who worked in the Bank of England. I had two small rooms with kitchenette up under the eaves. They were a lovely family and most hospitable. They had three glamorous daughters and a son and I was much envied by young colleagues and senior boys, though Yole kept an eagle eye on us all. I was playing quite a lot of bowls in the Guildford area and reached the quarter finals of the Surrey County Singles Championship, which had meant weekly matches throughout the season on a variety of bowling greens around the country. This gained me several games for the County Team and my Surrey County Badge. I was also playing for the London and Southern Counties team (in effect the MCC of Bowls) and for the London Welsh. The highlights of that season for the latter were the matches against London Scottish at Watney's Brewery green at Mortlake and against the London Irish at Guinness's – both very alcoholic occasions I must admit.

By now my brother Richard had become a don at Selwyn

College Cambridge and I was invited to a banquet there in November 1963. Sitting in his rooms late after a splendid evening he asked me what I intended to do in my career. I explained that I would so like to become a Housemaster but that at Charterhouse those appointments were made strictly in order of seniority and that although 31 at the time I was unlikely to become a Housemaster until my mid-forties, which seemed a long way off. 'Why don't you put in for a headmastership?' said Richard, 'I see in the papers that Hurstpierpoint is coming up next year.' I had never thought of such a move but after a splendid evening, which had terminated with port and an excellent cigar, it seemed an excellent idea! We roughed out a letter of application and I put as my referees Walter Hamilton, now Headmaster of Rugby, Brian Young and George Turner, a Governor of Charterhouse whom I had met several times at dinners in Brooke Hall. He was another remarkable Headmaster, who had been Master of Marlborough College and then Head of Makerere College in Africa before coming to Charterhouse as Headmaster for five years when Sir Robert Birley left and before Brian Young had been appointed. He was another of those great men of whom many tales have been, and still are, recounted when former pupils or colleagues or fellow heads meet together. My favourite is when as Headmaster of Charterhouse he had taken four school monitors to London for dinner. As they were driving home through South London – and he was a notoriously erratic driver – one of the boys plucked up the courage to say, 'Excuse me Sir, but we are still in the 30 mile limit' (George was driving at well over 50 mph at the time). 'Indeed I know that' came the reply, 'that is why I am driving as fast as I can to get out of it as quickly as possible.'

The finished letter read well and I retired to bed and slept soundly. When I surfaced the next morning I went round to my brother's rooms where he told me, to my unspeakable horror, that his scout (his manservant) had come in that morning and as was his custom had taken letters to the post and mine had been among them! I had not mentioned to my present Headmaster that I was putting in for a headship nor asked him if he would consider acting as referee – nor had I asked either of the other gentlemen. Panic set in and I returned in haste to Charterhouse and went immediately to see Brian Young. I did not mention the letter but merely asked his opinion of whether it would be a good idea for me to have a go. He had, of course, been appointed to Charterhouse at the age of 29 and when I replied to his question of 'How old are you?' '31', he said 'That seems to me a good age to try for it.' I wrote at once to Walter Hamilton and George Turner and having received very courteous and encouraging replies felt somewhat happier. It was then a question of waiting to see if anything might happen!

At the start of that academic year in September, Brian Young had summoned me to his study. 'Roger, you are the youngest Modern Language master here. As you know, I teach Italian O level in the Sixth form and I shall be leaving next Summer. (He had announced to our sorrow that he was leaving to be Head of the Nuffield Foundation.) I want you to sit in my classes and take O level next Summer. Then you can continue the teaching next September.' It was a daunting but flattering invitation and I agreed. Sitting in class with about a dozen of the brightest Carthusians was quite a strain but I survived until the start of the Cricket Quarter in 1964 by which time I had been offered the headmastership of Hurstpierpoint College. I therefore went to Brian's study and gracefully withdrew from attending his classes. Towards the end of May as I walked to my classroom I met a boy who said: 'You are first in for the oral exam, Sir.' I rushed to the noticeboards and saw my name there. I went to see Brian Young. 'I thought it would be good for you, Roger, and when you pass the O level you will almost certainly be the only member of the Headmasters' Conference with an O level. You are the youngest member and they will all be School Certificate men.'

I managed to bluff my way through the oral with much talk of Italian opera and later in the year sat the examinations – the first time I had sat in an examination room for 11 years. The tension was heightened by the fact that on one day I had to give an O level German Dictation to my form, then go to another classroom to be given an O level Italian Dictation, then back to my classroom to read an O level German story reproduction, and finally off to be given an O level Italian story reproduction and then have to try to write it down coherently. In late August I received a letter from Brian Young saying 'Well done. You passed the O level but one of the boys got better marks than you did.'

About February, I was told that I was on the short list for Hurstpierpoint and was invited to go down to visit the school and meet the current Headmaster. I had first met the Revd Canon Ronald Howard in 1951 when I was a Prefect at Lancing. The Woodard Headmasters of the Southern Division – Lancing, Hurstpierpoint, Ardingly and Bloxham – were having their termly meeting at Lancing and Frank Doherty asked the School Prefects to entertain the three visitors to tea – Ronnie Howard from Hurst was a terrifying figure, George Snow from Ardingly was immensely tall (I believe about 6ft 10 ins) and equally awe-inspiring, whilst the Headmaster of Bloxham, K.T. Dewey, was, more reassuringly, more like a robust farmer in appearance.

Now only thirteen years on I found myself walking up the driveway to the very imposing Headmaster's House and equally terrified at the thought of meeting him again. He opened the door to me himself. 'You must be Griffiths. Come in. I can't say I am glad to see you as I cannot bear the thought of handing over this school to anybody.' I was shown into a very elegant drawing room – he had a very specialized personal collection of English watercolours, and invited to sit down. 'Now ask me some questions.' – and my mind went a complete blank. After a few moments I said, 'Has this house got a good wine cellar?' For about half a minute, I felt that I had finished any chance of success, but he then said, 'No, it hasn't. But it should!' and roared with laughter and from that moment onward we got on well together.

Indeed, in a letter to Clifford Freeman, the Divisional Bursar, after our meeting, he wrote, 'Griffiths and I got on like a house afire.' I enjoyed the visit and found the school buildings delightful. The Headmaster's House seemed very large and I wondered how, if I were by any chance to be offered the appointment, I would manage to furnish it with my modest furniture from two small rooms chez Wilson. I did not meet any of the staff as it was during the school holidays, so the place seemed very quiet.

On the strength of two terms of learning Italian, Tony, Dick and I had decided to drive to Italy in the Easter holidays of 1964. We had negotiated hotels and garages with a great deal of arm waving and a certain amount of French and Latin. My triumph was at La Scala in Milan. We had arrived that day and found that Guiseppe di Stefano was singing in *L'Elisir d'Amore* by Donizetti. At the box office we were told that all seats had been sold. As we turned away a ticket tout came up and offered us three seats at double the price they normally were. I pointed out to him in my halting Italian that it was only half an hour to the start of the opera, that he probably would not sell the tickets and offered him about 10% above the cost of the tickets. He roared with laughter and agreed – so we went to La Scala, heard the great tenor and witnessed at first hand the rousing way in which an Italian claque functions.

About ten days into the holiday I had to leave the other two in order to return to London for the interview for Hurstpierpoint. They dropped me at Milan railway station and continued on their way alone. I got to London and spent the night at the Oxford and Cambridge Club and then at 1.50 p.m. presented myself at Brown's Hotel. I was the first candidate in after lunch. I learnt that there were six of us on this final short list but I did not know who any of the others might be. At two o'clock I was shown into a room. In the chair was the Bishop of Lewes, Provost of the Southern Division of the Woodard Corporation. The others were R.C. Freeman, the Divisional Bursar, Lt. General Sir John Evetts, Dick Thomas, a stained glass artist and Chairman of

Hurstpierpoint School Council, John Widdows, a solicitor and member of Hurst Council and Fairfax Scott, a don from Magdalene College Cambridge.

The Provost welcomed me and then invited Dick Thomas to ask me a question. 'Mr Griffiths, do you know anything about wine?' 'Well I have been Secretary of the Common Room at Charterhouse for six years and been responsible for buying all the wines for their entertaining. I also spent a year living in Paris and learnt a certain amount there, but I am still learning.' Second question, also from Dick Thomas, 'Do you intend to remain a bachelor?' 'No, but I do not intend to get married merely in order to gain a headmastership.' From John Widdows, 'Oh dear, what should I ask you? Mr Griffiths, do you know anything about vintage cars?' 'Well I have at present a 1936 Rolls and learnt to drive on a 1933 Rolls Park Ward saloon.' There followed a short discussion on cars and then Fairfax Scott: 'Mr Griffiths, we have heard about wine, women and cars. What do you know about education?' Taking my courage in both hands (or conversely being most naively foolish) I said: 'Well I failed my Dip Ed at Oxford and . . .' 'Good' said Fairfax Scott, 'I have never believed in these educational theories.' General Evetts: 'Mr Griffiths, what do you know about the science of engineering?' 'Well Sir John, not much. My first day as a boy at Lancing my Housemaster said to me Greek, German or Science and I chose German so my scientific knowledge is nil but I am fully in favour of all pupils having a basic knowledge.' 'Oh, you were at Lancing. I hadn't spotted that in your papers. So was I.'

The interview seemed to me to be going remarkably well. Then R.C. Freeman, the Divisional Bursar asked, 'Mr Griffiths, what do you know about finance?' 'Very little I must confess. I deal with the finances of the Common Room but that is about it. I have not had the responsibility of being a Head of Department or Housemaster with appropriate financial allowances. But I would expect to rely on the Bursar to keep me in the picture.' Provost: 'Why do you want to come to Hurstpierpoint?' 'My five and a half years at Lancing were immensely happy and I would like to be a member of the same foundation again.'

I was then asked if I had any questions to ask them but had nothing, so after some general chat the interview was over. I somehow felt that I had not made much of an impression. I went back to Godalming where my brother had come to stay the night. The next morning we were setting off for Wales. I thought I would just go to the Common Room to see if there were any letters, and there was one from R.C. Freeman offering me the headmastership!

There was a great celebration when we got home – though over the next few days I began to wonder just what I had actually done!

My last Quarter at Charterhouse passed peacefully and happily despite the O level Italian examinations! Brooke Hall needed a new staircarpet and so I put a different sample on each stair and invited colleagues to write down their choice when they arrived upstairs. Inevitably, there were so many different choices that I chose the one I liked best – and received from Brian Young the compliment: 'Roger, you are a born Headmaster!' I had greatly enjoyed being Secretary of the Common Room. The twice-weekly dinners and dinner with the Governing Body had given me great practice in arranging seating plans and indeed in constructing menus and finding appropriate wines. In the dining room, we had a set of eight eighteenth-century George III style chairs with eight matching Victorian reproductions and twelve smaller round-backed chairs. The year before, an extremely wealthy Old Carthusian had been invited to dine with us. After the meal he told me how much he had enjoyed the meal but said that it was the first time in 30 years that he had dined and sat on a chair without arms. He therefore proposed to give the Common Room a set of 36 matching carvers with the school crest embroidered on them. We really needed a new carpet for the dining room, but it was chairs or nothing, so we accepted them gratefully. Now to my good fortune, the Second Master, Ernest Fryer, asked me whether I needed any chairs for my new house and I was given the eight reproduction chairs and twelve round-backs for £4 a chair by the Common Room. They would have cost me, even in those days, a couple of thousand pounds, so I was immensely grateful and very fortunate.

I also scoured the antique furniture shops of that part of Surrey and acquired a dining table, tallboy and monk's cupboard and various other items over the next few months at Charterhouse. In those days it was possible to purchase large items of furniture at a more modest price than nowadays.

I telephoned Hurstpierpoint to ask Ronnie Howard if I could go down to visit and do some measuring up. His secretary informed me that he was busy (it was 2.00 p.m.) but would be available at 4.00 p.m. When I spoke to him he suggested that we should meet halfway between Charterhouse and Hurstpierpoint for our initial meeting as outgoing and incoming Headmasters. This we did and I had a very helpful meeting. About three weeks later, I needed to talk again and once again was told to ring after 4.00 p.m. I was then invited to the house with tape measure but was not allowed into the school or to meet anyone. I rang a couple of weeks later with a query and this time his secretary was out and I spoke to the school porter. 'Oh Sir, it is never any good telephoning between 2.00 p.m. and 4.00 p.m. as Canon Howard always has a rest after lunch.' Perhaps headmastering was not all go but one thing was certain – I was to inherit an excellent secretary.

I still had not met any of my future colleagues. My brother, Richard, was a Governor of Lancing College and a Fellow of the Southern Division, and he told me that they were meeting at Hurstpierpoint at the beginning of July. I told him of my wish to visit the school and he spoke to the Provost, who issued me with an invitation to that day. Ronnie Howard was very cross. 'I feel that as soon as you appear on the scene I shall appear redundant.' But he put a brave face on it and I was instructed to present myself at his house. When I arrived I was introduced to the Head Boy who, I found out later, had strict instructions <u>not</u> to let me out of his sight all day! The lunch was in part a disaster for me. The Bursar was taking around a jug of beer on a tray; as he arrived behind me the jug slid off the tray and I was soaked in beer! The Provost remarked, 'We don't normally baptize our new Headmaster in this way.' But to my embarrassment I was accompanied for the rest of the day by a heavy aroma of beer, which I hoped would not give my future pupils the wrong impression of me! I returned to Charterhouse feeling that I did at least have a better idea of the layout of the school but aware of the fact that at my start in September I was going to be very much in the dark as far as colleagues were concerned.

Ronnie had given me written comments on most of the staff which were very pithy and, in fact, very perceptive and his secretary gave me a staff photograph with their names attached so I had a certain amount of homework to do in the Summer holidays.

My last few days at Charterhouse were full of farewell parties, culminating in a splendid dinner in Brooke Hall. I had had seven wonderful years in a great school. I had made friends for life with various colleagues, I had taught some delightful pupils and had learnt a great deal about schoolmastering, notably from the Housemaster, Eric Harrison, whose House Tutor I had been. Now I had to face the future alone – my first task being to furnish the Headmaster's House and my most important task getting to know my future colleagues.

Chapter 9

THE HEADMASTER'S HOUSE looked very large and terrifying with not a stick of furniture in it. It was, in fact, an imposing building, which had been constructed in the 1930s for the then Headmaster, who had the top floor as rooms for the 13 servants he employed. Ronnie Howard as part of his great development plan for the College had turned the Sanatorium into a Junior School and a number of small boys now slept on the top floor of the house, whilst the first floor was occupied by the Sanatorium under the eagle eye of the remarkable Sister Berry. Thus my house was in effect a ground floor flat with a very large drawing room, immense entrance hall, study, single bedroom, bathroom, single guest room and at the back of the house, a bedroom/sitting room, bathroom and kitchen for the housekeeper I had to find.

This turned out to be difficult. The first lady I appointed lasted a fortnight and then told me she was leaving – no explanation but I believe that I had been used! She was filling in time between jobs as she left for another post. In despair, I telephoned Country Cousins, based in London, and told them what I needed. Two days later a small, trim, figure appeared in my drawing room. Kitty Taylor was about 4 ft 10 ins tall, smartly dressed with sheer silk stockings and high heeled shoes. She told me she was 63 and proceeded to interview me for about half an hour, at the end of which she announced that she could begin immediately. It was indeed a fortunate choice! She was one of the most remarkable characters I have ever met. I gradually learnt her life history. She had been an opera singer and had, in fact, sung the role of Musetta to Dame Nellie Melba's Mimi in *La Bohème* at Covent Garden in the first performance after the end of the First World War. She had sung with the Beecham Opera Company for some years. Her maiden name was Kitty Starling but Beecham, characteristically, had said that no-one in his opera company could possibly sing under that name. He christened her Destournel (the French for starling) and she sang for years under that name. I still have in my possession some old 80 rpm, one-sided, gramophone records of her singing (usually with flute obligato) some operatic gems. She had a very clear, bell-like tone. One of the great features of life with her as my housekeeper were the stories of some of the operatic greats of her generations.

On one occasion, I was listening to an LP of one of the greatest American sopranos when Kitty came in (she always claimed that 'Madam' as she always referred to Melba had taught her how to enter a room and it was certainly a dramatic event) – 'Who is that singing?' I replied 'It is the great Geraldine Farrar', to which came the comment, 'Oh, darling Geraldine, she always sang half a tone flat'! A couple of months later, she fell ill with 'flu. The school doctor came to see her. 'You must look after her, particularly in view of her age' She was, in fact, 83 and I had never realized it.

Kitty was a great cook and loved it when I gave dinner parties. I can still remember her walking around the house with cigarette in mouth and feather duster in hand, always missing the cigarette ash which trailed behind her. She remained with me for nineteen months but left when I got married – 'I have never in my life worked for another woman.'

When she left the opera stage, she had been in musical comedy for a time and then had a spell as visiting professor of voice production at the University of Berkeley, California – the Americans must have loved her! When she left Hurstpierpoint she went to London and looked after three bachelor masters at Westminster School for a time but then retired to live in Hove where she died in her early nineties.

As Ronnie Howard had not wanted me around while he was

still Headmaster, I now had to meet my new colleagues, and a remarkable group they were. The three most senior had been in the school since the early 1930s. Ken Mason, the Second Master, was a tower of strength to me as a new, and rather terrified, Headmaster. Ken was not only Second Master but also Senior Housemaster (he had been a Housemaster for 30 years), Head of History, Master-in-Charge of Careers and Master-in-Charge of Shooting. Robert Bury had been a Housemaster for almost as long, though had been absent on War service. He was Head of Classics, had produced the School Shakespeare play for 27 years and been Master-in-Charge of Cricket for almost as long. He also produced the school timetable each year. Robin Gregory had been a Housemaster for 29 years, was in charge of Biology and ran numerous societies and games in the School.

Ronnie Howard had left me details of the first day of term, including Housemasters' meeting at 11.00 a.m., full Masters' meeting at 12 noon. The Housemasters' meeting was quite an experience for one who had not been a Housemaster himself. Apart from the three mentioned above, there were George Lambert, who had been a Housemaster for 14 years at that time, Frank Florey, a similar length of time, William Alban, eight years and John Peters, 5 years with another 13 to go. The meeting was amiable and brief and I felt confident that I had a very good set of men with whom to work. At midday, I walked to the school Library – 27 men, all gowned, rose to their feet as I entered. I began by saying that we had not met but that I looked forward to working with them. I then gave out a few notices and then threw the meeting open for any comments or points to be made. No one said a word – and the meeting had only been going for 5 minutes. After a brief pause, I muttered my best wishes for a happy and successful term and we broke up. As I was leaving the Library, Ken Mason came up to me: 'Headmaster, you seemed surprised that no one spoke.' 'Surprised,' I replied, 'I was simply terrified.' 'Well you see, Canon Howard never liked anyone to raise any points in public. If we had something to say we made an appointment to see him and he then took his decision in his own time.'

This had been quite a contrast to staff meetings I had known before where, although the Headmaster was clearly in charge, all present were encouraged to participate and speak their minds. But I remembered advice from Brian Young. 'You will want to make changes but make them gradually and after consultation with senior colleagues so that they come and feel that they have a part in running the school – even when it is you who takes the decisions.'

I found that I was certainly in charge of the whole show. Every boy, including Second Year Sixth, had to have written leave signed personally by the Headmaster to go beyond the first bend in the road on each of the three roads leading from the College. A couple of days into that first term, a senior Housemaster came to see me with a 'major problem'. A boy in his House had very bad toothache but (and this was on a Monday) 'He will have to miss two lessons on Friday morning. That is the best I can do.' I said that regardless of what he was missing he should go immediately, or as soon as humanly possible, to the dentist and that I never wanted to be troubled with such trivia again. But the previous regime's orders continued. At my first annual meeting of The Headmasters' Conference that October I was summoned by the Secretary from a public session. Fearing that the school might have burnt down (as suggested by one or two helpful colleagues as I left the hall) I hastened to the telephone to find that a boy's father had died but that no one in the College would take the decision to let the boy go home – it had to be with the sole permission of the Headmaster!

Many years later when Membership Secretary of HMC I was, I hope, able to calm many a Headmaster who rang with a major problem in his school by telling him of my experience. One week into headmastering with no previous administrative experience behind me, the Master of the Junior School came to my study with 'a major problem'. Apparently, the Assistant Chaplain had been 'interfering' with small boys in the Junior School and when one had remonstrated had told him 'It is all right. The new Headmaster has instructed me to do this as part of a course on the facts of life.' I summoned the Assistant Chaplain – a man of my own age and a bachelor – to my study and accused him of this behaviour. He accepted it and I said: 'You are to be out of the College within one hour and I shall report this to the DFE.' He threw himself on the floor in front of me and said: 'If you send me away I shall kill myself.' – but I had no option. I must confess that for the next few days, every time the telephone rang my heart missed a beat. I had no one to talk to – I had not been in the school long enough to acquire a confidant. However, a couple of months later I was walking through the cloisters and met the man. To my demand as to what he was doing there, he replied: 'I was in the neighbourhood and thought I would look in to see some old friends.' My comment – 'Last time I gave you an hour to be out of the place – now it is five minutes before I call the police.' He is still on List 99 but it was a harsh introduction to the problems that may affect a Headmaster.

My Secretary, Marjorie Hooppell, was all that I had expected. She was an outstanding example of that most important breed who are the backbone of a school. During the war, she had been in Naval intelligence and she commanded the respect and admiration of everyone in the school. An example of her breadth of knowledge. After about a month at the school I received a letter in French and said to her that I would reply to it myself. 'Headmaster, I am perfectly capable of taking dictation in French', and after a couple of minutes during which I had been speaking slowly – 'and at the correct speed.' When the letter arrived on my desk for signature, every accent and agreement was correct. A similar thing happened some six months later over a letter received which was in German! To my great sorrow, she left on the morning of her sixtieth birthday, some seven years into my time at Hurstpierpoint, but she had steered me through many problems and difficulties with complete aplomb.

I had resolved not to make too many changes at first and during my first year I think there were only two of any significance. The first was to prohibit boys from using the cane. School Prefects had been allowed to beat miscreants and I did not believe this was right. My second change was to do away with the separate stiff white collars which all boys had to wear as part of the school uniform and which were a source of great discomfort, particularly to the thirteen year olds.

There had not been half-term breaks at the school for some years. It was the custom for the Headmaster at the morning Assembly to announce that the following day would be a half holiday to celebrate any particular event or success. This, I was told, had the great merit that the boys did not have the time to plan any great move away from the school so that we could still keep an eye on them. Rashly, I stood up in that first October and said: 'We will have a half holiday tomorrow to celebrate the forthcoming Conservative election victory. (Polling was that day.) The next morning, it was announced that Labour had won and numerous boys came up to ask whether the half holiday was now cancelled. I replied that it would go ahead but take the form of a wake! I soon decided that it would be in everyone's interest to start the process of half-term breaks and this was begun in 1965. Nowadays, (2001) things have very much changed of course and pupils are at home much more frequently.

I do think, however, that boarding is a beneficial way of life. It teaches boys to live with other people and get on with them, it teaches them to take responsibility for other people and for themselves and it teaches them really to appreciate their homes and families. Sadly, in a society where family breakups and divorce are far more frequent, it can provide a stability of environment which may be lacking at home.

On Prize Day in summer 1967, I said 'I suppose that this is perhaps the most difficult time in the history of the public schools to try to be a Headmaster.' The changes in schools and universities throughout the sixties and particularly the student unrest, were a constant source of worry. There was also a grave threat to the future of independent schools with the move to the left of the Labour Party. Between 1964 and 1979 there were only four years of Conservative Government and there was constant worry that the independent schools might be forced out of existence by legislation or financial constraints. The Labour Government pushed forward the idea of comprehensive education, increased tertiary education and in so many ways opened up a clear divide between state and independent sectors. There was the constant threat of removal of charitable status. Yet looking back on that period now, the political threat never actually materialized. We were left alone to continue as we were with the same status and the same examination system. Changes were to come later!

The 'revolution' was to be much more on the society within the schools themselves. Hurst had for many years been a 'monastic community' in outlook, keeping itself to itself. The boys of the late sixties were far more interested in how the school should be run – what they could change for themselves in the decision making process. Looking back on it, I think that the school had been an autocracy, though a benevolent autocracy.

Although changes were made, they did not to any great extent change that style of government. The boys – and staff – were listened to and felt that they had gained some advantages to their way of life, but in essence, the Headmaster was still in sole command. Over my first few years, the Sixth Formers gained many privileges. In 1965 we began a Sixth Form Union but their demands were limited to social changes. A Sixth Form Common Room was set up with television and coffee machine and individuals were allowed radios, record players and music centres in their studies and in 1970, a Sixth Form bar was introduced.

For those who preferred to relax by leaving the school buildings, all boys were allowed bicycles and bounds were enlarged to include Burgess Hill, Hassocks and Haywards Heath, though

Brighton remained out of bounds except with Housemaster's permission. In 1986, Sixth Formers were allowed to London or Brighton at weekends with parents' permission. Life did become more relaxed for pupils though there were the occasional misdemeanours.

I think that the role of Headmaster is immensely enjoyable though immensely difficult! I know that throughout my 22 years there were always those in the school who thought that life was still too disciplined and old-fashioned and those who thought that there was too much change and relaxation of rules. I tried to keep the best of the past whilst preparing boys for the very different world beyond the school. Certainly when I left it was a different place from the school I inherited, but many of the best features of that time had been maintained.

My first few terms were certainly the loneliest I had ever known and on many occasions as I sat alone in the Headmaster's House after my evening meal I wondered what I was doing. In November 1965 I stood up at a school Assembly and announced: 'We shall have a half holiday tomorrow to celebrate the fact that I am engaged to be married' – the best thing I ever did both for myself and for Hurstpierpoint College.

When I arrived, I found that there was a school appeal under way. It was being organized by a Captain John Brown, RN, who worked for the appeal firm Hooker Craigmyle. Sadly as a result of Canon Howard's illness in his last few terms the appeal had not progressed as well as was hoped. The target was modest – £64,000 – but as of September 1964 it stood at minus £300 as the firm had been paid their fee and the money had not come in! My first few months were spent in fundraising meetings around the country and we eventually reached the target – but inflation meant that it was not nearly enough. About a month into my time at Hurst, John Brown asked me if I would like to go to his home in Burgess Hill for Sunday lunch to discuss plans for the appeal. I went and met his wife and youngest daughter, Diana, who immediately struck me as most attractive. The afternoon was appeal business and after tea I said that I must be getting back to the school. To my astonishment, Diana said: 'Could I please cadge a lift with you? I actually work for you as I am Matron at the Junior House.' I was happy to oblige and for the next four months we managed to go out together despite the eagle eyes of boys, masters and Kitty Taylor.

In November 1965 I asked Diana to marry me and then went over to ask the permission of her parents. Their reaction was slightly off-putting. 'She is much too young to be the wife of a Headmaster.' said her mother. 'There are two things in life I don't like,' said her father, 'schoolmasters and Welshmen'. Despite which comments we were happily married on April 2nd 1966 and remain happily married now in 2002.

A few days later, the Bursar came to see me in my study. 'Headmaster, I think you know Miss Brown, don't you? She has just handed in her resignation. She is the best matron we have ever had in Junior House. Do you think you could persuade her to change her mind?' 'Oh no, Dick, one should never do that to anyone or you will never ever be able to get rid of them should that need arise.' It gave me great pleasure two days after the end of term to call him over to the study where Diana was with me and to say 'Dick you are the first person in College to know that we are engaged to be married!'

The wedding itself was in the College Chapel where we had the Provost, Lloyd Morrell, Bishop of Lewes, resplendent in yellow cope and mitre, Michael McAdam, the Chaplain and Howard Rose, the Vicar of Ditchling, the Brown family priest. Michael married us and Lloyd spoke and the College choir sang beautifully – they had come back specially despite being on holiday. The reception was in the Dining Hall at which in schoolmasterly fashion I read a 'report' on Diana and we were then driven by the School Porter, Mr Baker, to Brighton College where I had left my car for fear of decoration! We had a meal with Henry and Naida

April 2nd 1966.

Christie, our dear friends who ran Brighton College, and then left in my 1936 Rolls for Dover.

On a deserted sea front in Folkestone in pouring rain I was stopped by a police car. 'Do you know the speed limit here, sir?' 'I imagine on a road this size it is 40 mph.' 'No sir, it is 30.' 'Well I am sorry officer, I was doing 38.' 'You will be hearing from us, sir.' Diana said, 'Will it be soon – you see we were only married this afternoon.' This was ignored. On our return, I found a summons and a few weeks later the *Mid-Sussex Times* had the headline 'Headmaster had hastening to honeymoon hotel'.

This event did not spoil a wonderful honeymoon. We crossed the channel the following morning. Diana had warned me that she was a very bad sailor but I was terrified (quite irrationally) at the thought of flying. It was a very stormy morning but we got on board and I gave her 2 Kwells and 2 large brandies! About halfway across, Diana said 'I feel hungry' and we went below to have an excellent lunch – there was only one other person in the dining room. We reached France, got into the car and Diana fell asleep until we reached Reims, our destination for that night. Her Godfather, John Codner, had given us as a wedding present a cheque – 'to be spent on a good hotel and meal on your honeymoon'. The hotel was excellent and the meal outstanding, culminating in a large brandy each 'on the house' to celebrate our wedding.

We drove on to Bernkastel on the Moselle where our room had a balcony overlooking the river. Easter Day we were in Bonn and went to the Cathedral where soloists, choir and orchestra of the State Opera sang Beethoven's C Major Mass. It was standing room only in the Cathedral.

We crossed back to England on 16th April – in mid-channel it was snowing and when we arrived in Dover the roads were appalling. It took us twice as long as normal to get from Dover to Hurstpierpoint and we had to delay our visit to my parents in South Wales.

Peter King in his History of Hurstpierpoint College writes:

During his interview, Roger was told they were looking for a married man. He put this right when he married Diana Brown in the Chapel in April 1966, a marriage followed in time by the birth of three daughters Elizabeth, Helen and Caroline. Diana Griffiths proved to be the right Headmaster's wife in the right place at the right time. Hurst was more than a little misogynist in the early 1960s but no-one could maintain that attitude for long in her presence. Diana was the first Head's wife since Isabel Coombes to play an important and well-liked part in school life. She was involved in Chapel and school drama and was an excellent hostess not only to distinguished guests but to the boys and masters invited to the Headmaster's House. Diana clearly put the school first in her life and helped to make it plain that the Griffiths were a husband and wife Head's team.'

Chapter 10

WHAT A JOY IT WAS to have someone with whom to share the pleasures – and the problems – of headmastering! I said earlier that my first five terms in the hot seat were some of the loneliest of my life. Now there was someone to whom I could turn for advice, for support and for comfort. I suspect that I was very selfish in my demands but Diana was always there and always prepared to subordinate her own interests and needs to my demands and those of the school. And there were shared interests also, visits to the theatre and to concerts, holidays exploring the continent and parts of our own country. Diana's mother had been a principal singer with the D'Oyly Carte Opera Company before her marriage and still kept her hand in by producing the annual Burgess Hill Operatic Society Gilbert and Sullivan operetta. She would also help out with make-up at College drama productions.

In 1966 Robert Bury produced *A Midsummer Night's Dream*, with very elaborate sets designed by Francis Russell Flint, the gifted art master, and a boys only cast. I had an amusing first encounter with Russell Flint. He had, in fact, been the art master at Lancing when I was a boy there. His practice was to say at the start of a term, 'I am going to paint. If you wish to learn, watch and follow me; if you do not, then bring in a book and sit quietly at the back of the classroom.' When the Hurst masters lined up on my first day to meet me, I greeted him with the words, 'Don't you remember me? I sat at the back of your class at Lancing', to which his response was, 'Oh my God, I am seen through!' We had a very amusing couple of years together but he then decided to devote himself full-time to his painting and left. Sadly he was killed a few years later in a most unfortunate accident in France.

His successor was Arthur Morgan, who came for interview with much hair and full moustache. I pointed out to him that I would like to appoint him but that I was particularly determined to have the boys neatly presented and therefore expected masters to be the same. The day before the start of the next term, a young man in a suit presented himself in my study. I thought it must be a Sixth Former I had not yet met – it was Arthur Morgan complying with my wishes!

The whole question of hair length and appearance was one which dominated my first few years at Hurst. I found that I had inherited a system whereby once a month a team of barbers came into the school and took over two classrooms for a day. Then the whole school was timetabled through – and any boy who appeared untidy after that was sent back at the end of the day for a second trim. Canon Howard told a splendid story against himself. He was walking around the school and came across a very scruffy boy. 'Go to the village at once, have a haircut and report back to my study within the hour.' He returned to his study and the boy duly reported back. 'That's better. Now I can't remember your name or House. Remind me.' 'But Sir, I am not a member of your school. I am here with a visiting team from Lancing.' I do not think there were many Headmasters who could command such instant obedience. I certainly never managed it.

After some six months I stopped compulsory hair cuts for Sixth Formers and later also for Fifth Formers on the understanding that if I, or any master, felt that a boy looked untidy, he was to be sent immediately to the village barber. The result was a happier atmosphere in the school but at the same time a very different appearance to the boys and looking at old photographs I now realize how much standards were allowed to slip during the late sixties and early seventies. Crew cuts presented more difficulties, for it takes time to grow hair! Brightly coloured hair styles were, however, never allowed.

Questions of various types of footwear, drainpipe trousers,

jewellery, remained with us for a decade or more and we spent hours at Housemasters' meetings and during the days battling to keep up standards as we saw it. Were we right to attempt to preserve an old attitude in the face of changes in society? I think that at least our efforts had the merit of ensuring that our pupils still gave a reasonable appearance to the outside world – and it actually gave the boys plenty about which to grumble which perhaps kept them from some of the further excesses of youth in the society of that time.

But to return to the drama scene. After the performances of the Shakespeare play, Robert Bury announced that that was to be his last production. He had produced the Shakespeare play for 21 years so this was an understandable decision but it was understandable also that no other member of the Common Room was prepared to take it over. The Shakespeare Society was the oldest in any school in the country with an unbroken record since 1858, apart from a few War years. The elaborate sets and rather stylized acting seemed to be in need of change, however, and so no one came forward in 1966. I undertook, on the strength of my experiences at Charterhouse, to produce *King Lear* with a very modern stage setting, modern music and three girls from the Burgess Hill School for Girls as the daughters of Lear. It certainly was a change and opened the way for much more drama on the Hurst stage. Robert Bury's comment was, 'I enjoyed it Headmaster, but I still prefer boys to girls in Shakespeare.' The following year, Arthur Morgan produced the play and then I did again in 1969, 1970 and 1971. Bill Alban, a very accomplished actor himself then took over as Director of Drama to be followed by Neil Morris who had been a pupil in the school and who had been Malvolio in my production of *Twelfth Night*. My most ambitious production was *Othello*, again with girls 'borrowed' from Burgess Hill.

I knew full well how Common Room plays or productions were not only very popular with pupils but were also a very good means of strengthening the unity within a Common Room from

HMS Pinafore: Captain, author; Dick Deadeye, Christopher Dean.

my Charterhouse days. I therefore suggested at the start of the Michaelmas term 1969 that we should as a Common Room put on *The Pirates of Penzance* by Gilbert and Sullivan. Bill Alban made a magnificent Pirate King and there were several Housemasters among his band of pirates, a great line-up of policemen and a bevy of wives as the daughters of Major General Stanley, a part which I took myself. The College orchestra accompanied us splendidly and a good time was had by all. Some four or five years later we produced *HMS Pinafore* when as the Captain, I had, to the school's joy, the fun of addressing my wife (Buttercup) as 'a plump and pleasing person'. Our last Gilbert and Sullivan offering was *Trial by Jury* in 1980. By this time I was finding it more and more difficult to remember lines so the part of the Judge enabled me to have my script on the bench in front of me but unseen by the audience. These Common Room ventures encouraged many more theatrical productions to take place, including Anouilh's *Becket* (in the Chapel) and Elliot's *Murder in the Cathedral*, both produced by

Oliver: Mr Bumble, Neil Page; Mr Brownlow, author.

Christopher Dean, who also in 1970 devised and produced a Pageant of the College History which has been revived successfully on several occasions since. Individual Houses also began to put on plays of a wide variety and, of course, now that the school is fully co-educational, there is full scope for more and more to take place. The Junior School also under its Master, Robin Paul, put on some splendid productions in the years 1972-1985.

One of the most memorable, in which I was invited to take part, was the musical *Oliver*. I was cast as the 'benevolent old gentleman' Mr Brownlow, which could perhaps shed a kind glow over the role of Headmaster. The production was a great success.

The theatre, which was built in 1956, has quite recently been modernized and upgraded and named the Bury Theatre in memory of one who gave so much to the history of theatre in the College over the years. It is interesting that whereas in the late sixties the boys seemed to lose interest in many of the societies which were then in existence, by the early seventies new societies and interests had emerged and there is now a tremendous variety of opportunity available for all pupils.

I have already noted the long service of the Housemasters which I found when I arrived. There was no specific period of time for holding a housemastership and it soon dawned on me that perhaps one reason some of them had remained in post so long was that a Housemaster had an allowance of £100 per annum for that work, which was a considerable help when the actual salary scale was very modest indeed. At my second Governors' meeting I asked for permission to say that any Housemaster who had completed 15 years in post could relinquish it but retain the Housemaster's allowance. There were plenty of other administrative posts I could find them which would justify the continuing payment. The fact that five Housemasters had left their Houses in the next four and a half years proved my point. It also meant that there were clear chances of promotion for younger members of the Common Room.

Robin Gregory had completed 30 years as Housemaster of Star House by 1965. He was a gentle and shy man, a scientist and very distinguished French Horn player and he felt it was time to relinquish the House. He remained a loyal member of staff until his sudden and unexpected death in 1971.

About a month after my arrival at Hurst, it was brought home to me how every move and action of a Headmaster is on public display and noticed by everyone. Robin and his wife Margaret had invited me to their home for an evening meal. I arrived and Robin asked me what I would like to drink. Before I had time to reply, Margaret's voice came from the kitchen, 'Don't be silly, you know he drinks gin. That's why you bought the bottle'. I hoped that my reputation was not too bad throughout the school.

The most important persons in a school as far as the Head-master is concerned were the Second Master, the Chaplain, the Bursar, the Chairman of Governors and the Headmaster's Secretary. I have already spoken of Kenneth Mason, the Second Master. He had devoted his whole life to Hurstpierpoint. He had come to the school in 1933 and after a year in charge of the Junior House became Housemaster of Fleur de Lys in 1934, a post he held until 1960. (From 1940-1945 he also looked after Red Cross House while Robert Bury was away on War service). In 1960 he became Housemaster of the newly built Martlet House. He was a highly successful head of history, had commanded the OTC/CCF and ran hockey, squash, shooting and careers. His wife Peggy had been a gracious hostess for my predecessor when needed and had also devoted herself totally to the school with her husband. Their son, James, was my first Head Boy. I could not have had a more solid support in my early years and though he retired in 1973 is still as I write this, active and alert, still perfectly capable of driving himself to any function at the College and still much respected and admired by Old Boys and former colleagues.

In a Woodard School, I had been brought up to accept at Lancing the Chapel as the centre focus of the community and of course that was the thinking behind Woodard's whole concept of education, particularly in a boarding school. The Chapel at Lancing is, of course, built on the grand scale to be the cathedral of the Woodard Corporation. But as in all the schools, he built the Chapel at Hurstpierpoint on the grand scale. There is a grand series of steps up to the High Altar and the school sit in collegiate fashion facing each other.

The Chaplain, Michael McAdam, had been two years senior to me at King's College Cambridge and was, like myself, a Modern Linguist. He was certainly one of the best school Chaplains I have ever met. He was liked and respected by everyone in the Hurst community and my years working with him were of the happiest, though I must say that I was equally fortunate with his successors.

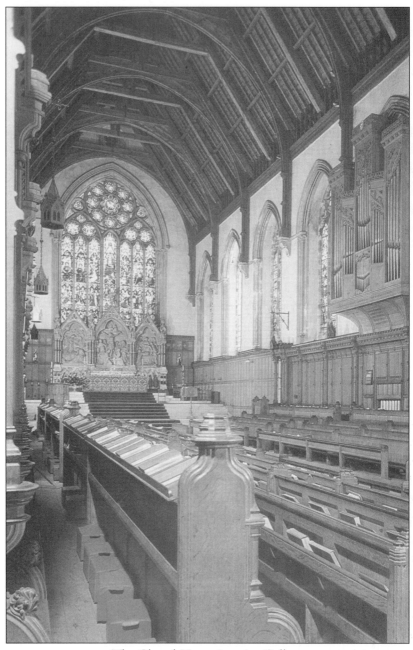

The Chapel Hurstpierpoint College.

The Bursar, Dick Evans, was a very nice person. He had had quite a difficult time with Ronnie Howard, as Ronnie had been his own Bursar for the first fifteen of his nineteen years and then the Governors had said that he should have a Bursar. I think that a Bursar has a very difficult role to play in a school. He has constantly to say no to people who want or need something involving finance which the school may not have. He has to keep his Headmaster in check when the latter has grandiose ideas for enlarging or improving the school. And he has to try to maintain a happy atmosphere – and to make sure that the buildings and plant generally remain in good order. Dick was very easy to work with and here again I was fortunate.

The Chairman of Governors, Dick Thomas, was a stained glass artist and a very intelligent and cultivated man. He would come to stay the night before a Governors' meeting and go through the agenda with me, finding out what conclusions I wished to have. Then at the meeting, to my astonishment, he would in the morning lead the Governors towards decisions which were diametrically the opposite to those which we had discussed the previous evening. In the afternoon session he would gradually manipulate discussion so that by the end of the meeting all had come round to what he and I had decided before. It was nerve-wracking for me but he confided to me that he enjoyed manipulating people! He was a good Chairman because he was a good listener and because he was a source of the best possible advice when I had a problem. Almost his first words to me were, 'There are two vacancies for Governors and I thought you might like to choose them in order to have a couple of friends in the right place.' This was a very civilized attitude but in fact in all my 22 years I never had any major problems or disagreements with any of my Governors. He retired after two years as my Chairman and they elected one of my nominees, Sir Richard Mathias, an Old Etonian stockbroker and family friend, who had been a code breaker at Bletchley Park during the War and who was an equally wise guide and friend to me.

My secretary, Marjorie Hooppell I have written about already. The post of Headmaster's Secretary is a key one in the running of the school. She had the respect, admiration and affection of everyone in the place and I was extremely fortunate to have her at my right hand for my first years in post.

So – all the key figures in the school were friendly and positive and I now had the enormous benefit of happy family life as well.

Diana knew the school of course after her work in the Junior House. We both enjoyed entertaining and she was, and still is, a marvellous cook. We began by entertaining all the teaching staff and their wives to dinner. We also had the school prefects to dinner twice a term. Then each Sunday there were the visiting preachers to entertain and on Saturdays there might be a lecturer or musician who was to give a recital to the school and outside visitors. In this way we met a number of very special people some of whom became permanent friends. One of these was the great singer Ian Wallace. When we got back to the house after his recital, Diana met us with the words, 'I have just been watching you on the TV and now here you are!' 'I have never seen myself on TV' said Ian, 'May I go and watch it?' So we had supper on our knees in front of the set and it was a joy to watch the expression on his face.

This was in 1967 and Diana had not been able to come to the concert as she was babysitting. Our first daughter, Elizabeth, had been born on the 19th December 1966. Two days before that was the end of term Carol Service and Brian Thomas had come to stay the night. We had dined and breakfasted alone as Diana had already gone into Cuckfield Hospital for the arrival of the baby. I had the great joy of being present when Elizabeth was born and can still remember the amazing sensation it produced in me. Mother and daughter were home in time for Christmas and then we took the new member of the family to South Wales to meet her grandparents.

We were still living at Hurst in what was essentially a bachelor flat. We occupied the small single bedroom which I had had when

I arrived and which could just about contain a double bed but nothing else whatsoever. The small single guest room was now to be a room for Elizabeth but it soon became clear that living conditions were bleak. We therefore took over the dining room as our bedroom and moved the dining table into the very large hall. This was not by any means ideal from the point of view of entertaining but it did give us a bit more private space. I pointed out to the governors that conditions were not in any way satisfactory and when we found that a second child was on the way they agreed finally that the first floor of the house (converted by Canon Howard into the school Sanatorium when he turned the existing San. into the nucleus of the Junior House) should be given back to the Headmaster and family and that a new Sanatorium should be build in the Headmaster's garden across the road.

A disadvantage was that we no longer had a private garden – the small lawn outside the front door was enclosed by a hedge for us but it was a very public garden as everyone entering or leaving the school passed by it. However, it was a joy to have a proper dining room once again and a fine bedroom looking south to the Downs, together with a proper room for the children and a good size double room for guests. When the Bursar was showing us around what was to be our home, we found in the bathroom two small school type baths side by side (patients for the use of). We commented to him how charming it would be to bath side by side but they were removed and a proper bathroom suite was installed! Helen, our second daughter, arrived on February 16th 1968, and we now had a double helping of fun – and problems! Before marriage, I had had a resident housekeeper, daily help, someone to wait at dinner parties and the services of a gardener. When Diana appeared, all of these disappeared meaning that she had an immense amount to do. With two small children in the house she needed help and we found daily help for her. We then decided to invest in the services of an au pair girl.

Beatrice was very French and did not, I think, take over kindly to the work involved with small children. The idea of being in a community which was 95% male obviously appealed, however. Some weeks after her arrival a very embarrassed Second Master came to see me to inform me that she had the habit in the evening of not fully closing the curtains of her room (which faced towards the main school building) and placing a red candle in the space provided. 'Which, Headmaster, does not perhaps convey the right attitude to young members of staff or to the senior boys.' I had to speak to Beatrice about this which she did not really accept. On another occasion, thinking that she was in her room, I locked up the front door as we went to bed. On coming down the next morning I found a note lying on the front doormat. 'I could not get in and so I am sleeping with Mr Hill' – a married Housemaster who lived just opposite with his wife and family and to whom she had gone in dismay after failing to make herself heard at the front door! She was with us for about six months when we parted by mutual agreement but we did not venture a second time into the au pair world.

I had taken over a school with a staff many of whom had been in the place for some years. At first, I worried that they would not welcome a new young Headmaster. In point of fact, it was the relatively small number of young men on the staff who were not so happy. I have said earlier that I was determined not to make too many changes until I had settled in and been accepted by the staff and boys. This policy appealed greatly to the senior members of staff who were settled in their ways and did not like change. The younger men, who had been wanting some chances of earlier promotion and changes to the whole system were not so impressed and some moved on, which gave me the chance to make some appointments of my own. Some of the earliest were to devote the whole of their teaching career to Hurst. Notable among these were David Hughes, an old boy of the school, who was appointed in 1965 as Head of Economics and who over the next 32 years

The Hurst Common Room 1973: seated from l. to r. – H.R. Thomas; R.T. Ruddock; H.R. Holloway; R.W. Bury; K. Mason; author; G.E. Lambert; S.F. Florey; J.H. Peters; W.M. Alban and Sister Winifred Berry.

became a Housemaster and then Second Master, who set up the beginnings of what became and still is, the outstanding Careers Department and who also ran the rugby for a few years and was also in charge of the timetable for the whole school. Nicholas Searls, an old boy of Lancing, joined in 1967 and is still there as I write this. He began as Assistant Director of Music and in 1976 succeeded Neil Page, who went on to Malvern College and then to Uppingham, as Director of Music. Under Nicholas, the music really flourished and for twenty years a consistently high standard remained. The end of each Summer Term saw a series of varied music weeks and there were also choral and orchestral events, and visits from distinguished outside professional musicians. By the 1980s the Chapel Choir had given Hurst a musical reputation nationally and in 1983 they won the National Schools Choir Competition. They made four long-playing records over the years and successfully led the Chapel services, which were attended by many parents and friends. Nicholas gave up being Director of Music in 1996, but remains on the staff as a Housemaster and is still involved with the music making.

The Chapel has always meant a great deal to me. From my earliest time at Lancing in the late 1940s I had been involved in the worship, firstly as a treble in the choir and later as a Sacristan. I found on arrival at Hurst that I was fully committed to the way the Chapel services were conducted. At that time there was a short service each weekday and a major Sunday service attended by everyone, which alternated between a Sung Eucharist and Evensong. The school sang lustily and participated fully, a notable occasion being March 8th 1981 when the school's evening service was broadcast live by the BBC.

I was fortunate throughout my time at the College to have a succession of outstanding Chaplains. Michael McAdam, my first, was a pillar of strength, liked and admired by both staff and pupils, and his successors, Timothy Ganz and Gerald Buss, maintained the High Church atmosphere which to me was the essence of a

Woodard School. I think that it was the strength of character of these men, together with the genuine support of the vast majority of the Common Room and their families, that meant that even in the 1980s we still had the wholehearted support and participation of most of the boys. I only had a slight mishap with one clerical appointment. I had chosen a man who did not have experience of schools and schoolboys. Halfway through his first – and only – term with us, he presented himself at my study with a doleful expression and a bucket in his hand. It appeared that he had put this bucket outside the Porter's Lodge with a notice on it which read: 'Spend a penny here for Shelter' (a well known charity) and inevitably one of the boys, or more likely several, had taken him at his word and done just that! But as I have said my other appointments to the post of Chaplain were very successful.

In this I was fortunate in having Lloyd Morrell as Provost, followed by Mark Green, the former Bishop of Aston. Under Woodard's scheme for his schools, the Chaplains were appointed by the Provost and not the Headmaster, which could, and sometimes did, lead to major problems. Both Lloyd and Mark took the line that I should interview and choose and then present my candidate for their approval, which was most satisfactory from my point of view. Woodard himself had written of what he saw as the menace for the future well-being of the country of an irreligious education system. In the preamble to the Statutes of his Foundation, he wrote: 'I implore the civil government of whatever sort it may be to respect the rights of property and of conscience and not to set aside these my statutes which are given to secure the teaching of the Christian faith, pure and unadulterated, as we in England now enjoy it.'

It was a source of great joy to me that so many parents came to attend the Sunday Sung Eucharists. With the school numbers being high, we had to place seats for visitors on both sides of the main aisle facing each other, which just enabled the choir to make its way through, as well as seats in the anti-chapel behind the screen. On most Sundays all these seats would be filled by families, which gave a great sense of family atmosphere to the proceedings.

At the end of my first term at Hurst, we had a Christmas Carol Service on the last day. To my sorrow I found that in order to accommodate visitors we had to seat the lower two forms and their parents in the school library with the service relayed to them there. After consultation with Michael McAdam we decided together that in future years we would have two Carol Services, one on Advent Sunday and one at the end of term. As we had both been at King's College Cambridge, the format of the Advent Carol Service was obvious to us. It took the form of a procession from the cloisters through the West end of the Chapel to the High Altar with pauses for readings by boys from different year groups, a master, the Chaplain, a Housemaster and myself. The whole Chapel was lit only by candles and many candles were also carried in the procession. Candles were put on long stands along the window ledges above the stalls with a boy armed with a candle-snuffer perched on each windowsill to guard against any mishaps. It sounds fairly horrific, but in fact it made a truly memorable sight and the Advent Service over the years became a more desirable service to attend than the Christmas one. Fire precautions and regulations have meant the disappearance of those candles above the stalls but it is still a memorable sight with the whole of the East end appearing a blaze of light around the High Altar. I attended the 25th anniversary of this service last year and was as moved by it as ever.

Chapter 11

ONE OF THE MOST important tasks for a Headmaster is to build up relationships with preparatory schools and over the years I made this a strong feature of the way I tried to run the school. Sussex has always been a very flourishing area for preparatory schools, most notably along the coast between Brighton and Hastings. I have never enjoyed making speeches nor indeed preaching sermons, but I felt it was necessary to accept every invitation that came my way.

Indeed, even before I took up my post at Hurstpierpoint I had had the nerve-wracking (for a total non athlete) ordeal of judging a sports competition. Whilst still at Charterhouse, in my last term, I received a letter, more in the form of an imperial command, to judge the sports and present the prizes at Aldro School near Godalming. The letter came from Mrs Hill, widow of the founder of the school and a very formidable old lady indeed. I sought advice from my good friend Bernard Hanauer who ran the PE and some of the sport at Charterhouse and with the Lord on my side managed to bluff my way through a very difficult afternoon. It was a delightful school though and over the years we built up a good partnership so that each year a few boys would come on to us and they were always well prepared and delightful.

I was invited to another school to preach during my first year at Hurstpierpoint. Very nervous I arrived in good time and was met by the elderly Headmaster. 'Could I see the Chapel so that I can get my bearings?' I asked. 'No, the choir are practising there' came the reply. 'Where does the sermon come in the service?' 'After the anthem, if there is one; other than that it will probably be after the second hymn. Don't worry, I will turn around and wink at you.' By now I was becoming almost paranoid. We walked over to the Chapel just before the service was due to start. 'You walk in in front of me' was the instruction to me. 'How will I know where to sit?' 'Don't worry, I will give you a push in the right direction.' I somehow survived this ordeal which was only matched a few months later at another school where as we walked into the vestry my host said to me, 'By the way, I play the organ for the service so you will be taking it. I have put all the instructions on the pew in front of you.' After a few of these experiences it became less of a worry to preach in my own school Chapel, though I never fully conquered the feeling of panic as we approached that part of the service where the sermon occurs. My only solace was the comment made to me in the vestry on one occasion by a visiting bishop. 'I am always so nervous before I get into the pulpit but you know if you ever stop being nervous you will be over-confident and the result will not be a successful sermon!' To hear this from one whom I would have expected to be a real professional was certainly an encouragement.

Over the years I visited many preparatory schools and also a number of senior schools. At Ardingly, I sat at the West End with the Headmaster in his stall. The Head Boy came to collect me for the long walk to the pulpit. As we progressed eastwards I was somewhat astonished to see a large number of boys leaving the Chapel by the side aisle. On my return to the Headmaster's stall after the ordeal, he whispered to me, 'Sorry, I forgot to warn you that the choir are excused sermons as a thank you for all the work they do.'

But not all sermons were as nerve-wracking though. I still remember as I processed into Lancing Chapel behind the choir the realization that came to me that there were at least half a dozen men present who had taught me and who were fully aware of all my limitations. Visiting preachers to Hurstpierpoint were usually a joy as it was a chance for me to invite either old friends or distinguished clerics whom we could entertain afterwards, though even here there were the occasional hiccups. I had at his request invited Canon Alfred Woodard, grandson of the founder, to preach to us. He was then approaching 90 years of age and began his sermon with the words, 'I first visited Hurstpierpoint 73 years ago this month to run in a cross-country match against you.' I was aware of the school working out what age he could be. After ten minutes he suddenly said, 'I asked your Headmaster how long I should preach for and he said about 10 minutes, but I am going on so yah boo Headmaster!' The whole school turned to look at my pew to see my reaction – which was to laugh.

On another occasion, we had an elderly retired bishop, the brother-in-law of a member of the Common Room to preach. He launched into his sermon and after 27 minutes used the words 'and now...'. Before he could continue, the Chaplain leapt to his feet and announced the hymn but the old man waved him down and went on for another seven minutes. At least it gave the boys something to talk about and I have no doubt that some were running a book on the length of the sermon.

On the whole they made a good congregation. They would always give a preacher their attention for at least three minutes but if he had not grasped their imagination by then they would quickly switch off and sit (quietly I am glad to say) for the rest of the sermon but for those of us in the congregation who knew them well it was quite clear that they were not listening in the very slightest. I think that over the years I was able to grasp this when visiting other school Chapels and there were one or two occasions when my sermon was much shortened as I went along. I do believe most firmly, however, that ten minutes are quite long enough for a school sermon and that seven are about the right time for a senior school and five for a preparatory school.

On one occasion I had preached at a preparatory school on the theme of the ant and the grasshopper and introduced a third category – the dormouse – who did not really do anything at all. As I walked out of the Chapel at the end of the service through the assembled school and parents, the Headmaster's wife, a short, stout and very delightful person, said to me in a voice which was audible to the whole congregation, 'I think upon reflection that I am a rather stout grasshopper.'

Preaching and prize giving were the ideal ways of visiting and getting to know preparatory schools and their Headmasters. A good way to catch the attention of a prize day audience with a possible age range of 4 to 80+ (visiting grandparents), was to tell a story of the man who was invited for a weekend shooting in the countryside but told to bring his own dog. As he did not own one, he rang the nearest kennels to hire one and was told, 'We have an excellent dog here called Schoolmaster. He is quite the best gundog in Sussex and it will cost you £50 for the weekend.' The man thought this rather a lot of money but took the dog, paid and had a wonderful weekend's shooting. A couple of weeks later he was invited again and rang the kennels. 'Yes indeed, but Schoolmaster is now the best gundog in the South of England and it will cost you £100'. The man thought this a great deal of money but took the dog, paid and had another superb weekend. A while later he received another invitation and in some trepidation rang the kennels and asked how much now to hire Schoolmaster. 'Oh,' said the kennel owner, 'You can have him for a couple of quid.' 'Why, what has happened?' asked the man. 'Oh some idiot took him out and by mistake called him Headmaster,' came the reply, 'and now all he does is to sit on his backside and bark at people.'

Towards the end of a speech I would look at the youngest pupil in the front row and say to him, 'Now I am going to say a word about the most important person in the school. Who do you think that is?' The reply would inevitably be 'The Headmaster' to which I would reply, 'Oh no indeed. The most important person in the school is Mrs ......, (naming the Headmaster's wife) because she not only looks after all the people in the school including the cook and matrons but also keeps the Headmaster happy so that he is nice to you and everyone else.' This in fact I did and do believe most strongly and it was remarkable how often after the speech I was thanked for this and not only by the Headmaster himself but also by countless parents present.

One prep school I visited I found that every child in the school was to be given a prize for something, a feat which clearly took the Headmaster and his Secretary quite a while to construct reasons for the prize giving. There were about 180 pupils and so there was quite a long session of handshaking and then to my horror I found that there was a photographer present to take a photograph of me with each prizewinner as I gave the prize. My smile became a fixed grimace by the end of it and to crown it all, the photographs were displayed around the school during the afternoon in which I looked a complete nut case.

There is a certain art to presenting prizes. I was at a prizegiving at a school of which I was a Governor when the visiting VIP not only spoke individually for a full minute to each prizewinner (and there were 60+ of these) but then spoke himself for nearly an hour so that the Headmaster had to reduce his annual 'state of the union' message by about three-quarters of its length and we were still over half an hour late for lunch! I think that it is always worth having a few jokes in the speech provided that they are appropriate to the occasion. One which always appeals to the pupils and parents and probably to the assistant staff is, 'You know that if the Headmaster/Headmistress is the shepherd of his/her flock, the Second Master/Mistress is the little crook at the top of his/her staff'.

I used also to invite the Heads individually to come to spend a day at Hurstpierpoint with their wives, on which occasions I would get any former pupils of theirs now in my school to show them around and generally entertain them. Although not a games player myself, I also instituted a start of cricket season match for the First XI against the Headmaster's XI, in which my team consisted of local prep school Headmasters who had gained honours in the cricketing world at university or club or county

level together with two or three senior school Heads, such as Bill
Blackshaw from Brighton College, John Eggar from Shiplake and
Ken Shearwood from Lancing (not a Head but a great sportsman
and cricketer who had taught me when I was a boy there).

John Eggar was a delightful man. In one match he went in last
for our team who needed 12 runs to win in the last over. John
played the first three balls quietly and then hit a 2, a 4 and a 6 to
win the match for us on the last ball. The school cricket Captain
approached him, 'Sir, that must be the most memorable innings
you have played.' 'The second' replied John, 'the first was when I
made 212 not out for Derbyshire against Yorkshire at Headingley.'
In another match, the Headmaster's XI had made 215 and the boys
were 212 for 9 and going strongly with the last player in. A good
lunch and a hot afternoon were taking their toll of the older
players. Mike Gover, from the Dragon School, came up to bowl.
The ball travelled upwards and landed halfway down the pitch.
The umpires ordered the fielders to stand still and told the
batsman to walk from his crease and hit the ball. He took an
almighty swing, missed and fell over, whereupon Michael Ricketts
(Sutton Valence) leapt onto the ball and threw it to Ken Shearwood
the wicket keeper who whipped the bails off and we had won! The
boys thought it most unfair and in fact the Captain of Cricket
wrote to Wisden for a ruling but it was judged in our favour.

Somehow we always had a fine day and a great occasion. Diana
would invite the wives and families of my team for the day and we
always had a splendid party in our garden in the evening.

A couple of years after I had arrived at Hurst, we began an inter
prep schools athletics sports day and from a first beginning of some
six schools participating it gradually developed until we had teams
from over twenty schools participating with tremendous support
from their parents, staff and pupils. The event has now been
included in the IAPS national athletics event, and last year I
understand that thirty schools sent teams.

We also had inter prep school six-a-side hockey tournaments, and inter prep school art and verse speaking competitions. In these ways we encouraged prep schools and their parents to be aware of the existence of Hurstpierpoint College and built up connections with many of them – and they were also fun days though some of the visiting staff would get very over-excited on occasions.

Within the school itself, various new sports had emerged and continued to do so over my first ten years. These included badminton, fencing, golf, judo, canoeing, sailing and water polo, though most of them remained minority sports with the rugby, cricket, hockey and gradually athletics as the traditional major sporting activities. I was fortunate to find members of the Common Room to run these various activities and also a number of new societies flourished. There was no doubt however, that just as society outside the school walls was changing rapidly during the late 1960s so were attitudes within the school itself. Indeed I remember that on Prize Day 1967 I said to the assembled parents, 'I suppose that this is perhaps the most difficult time in the history of the public schools to try to be a Headmaster.' Certainly the unrest in the universities made its effect on schools across the country but looking back on that time I think that we at Hurst managed to avoid most of the extravagancies which were abounding. It is difficult when attempting to 'steer a middle course' to avoid the accusation of being old fashioned and head in the sand. Changes there were – one has only to look at photographs of sports teams of the period to see that long hair had descended upon the school in profusion. Many hours were spent (some might say wasted) at Housemasters' meetings in endless discussions on length of hair, width of trouser leg, on what of the generally hideous fashions of the day we were prepared to tolerate and what were definitely banned within the school. But the perpetual battle was worth it and I could still be relatively happy with the appearance of my school – I have always been and still am, a firm believer in the fact that boys need to have a set of rules and standards by which they should live and which enables them to have something to rebel against in the certain knowledge that if they are caught breaking a rule they know that they will be punished and they know what the punishment will be. I have never been a believer in corporal punishment and it was, in fact, rarely used and gradually disappeared completely but there are plenty of effective deterrents which one can use, particularly in the context of a boarding school where the pupils are or can be permanently on campus.

Rules on the bounds within which pupils should remain and on the number of home visits that could be made in the course of a term were gradually relaxed – but could still be enforced firmly on the miscreants. Throughout all this time I was most fortunate in the calibre of school prefects and head boys I had. I had inherited a group who firmly held to the privileges and powers of a previous era. Gradually, though quite quickly, we moved to a more caring but still firmly structured system of government. I suppose that I could be criticized for maintaining a somewhat feudal system wherein I was in charge and regulated any changes that might occur, but it produced a generally harmonious and settled community. We introduced a bar for the Sixth Form, the rules of which I based on the system we had used at Charterhouse (though I took care not to acknowledge the provenance of the rules – harking back to a previous school can be a fatal error for a Headmaster). There was a young master in charge but essentially it was run by the prefects with the full knowledge that any abuse of the system could mean the abolition of the enterprise.

No cash was exchanged. Members purchased vouchers from their Housemasters and as there was no treating of other members allowed, a check could be kept on how much a boy was consuming. There was a limit of two pints at any session per person. I think that nowadays I would allow the sale of wine but then it was only beer and cider with definitely no spirits. The system worked and the boys responded well.

It was interesting that about that time (1968) some schools were

The School and House Prefects 1970. 1967

141

The School Prefects and Bumble (12 weeks old) 1980.

introducing smoking rooms for senior boys. I asked the prefects for their views on such a move and it was unanimously agreed by them that it was not a good thing. In the words of one of them, 'If you allow smoking they will be looking for some other rule to break and the next move would be drugs'. I was, as I said earlier, very fortunate in the calibre of senior boys I had. The fear of drugs was something which developed very rapidly in the early 1970s and the proximity of Brighton was not a comfort. No Headmaster has in my opinion every been able to declare with hand on heart, 'There are quite definitely no drugs in my school' but I do believe that the staff and prefects were very much on my side in the vigilance they maintained in such matters. One unfortunate incident at the time, which played into my hands, had a fortunate effect. A Sixth Former had finished his A levels and had gone, with permission, into Brighton. I was in my study when a prefect came to tell me that a member of the school was rushing around the buildings screaming and stark naked! I learnt later that the unfortunate boy had been approached by a drug pusher in Brighton who sold him one Ecstasy tablet to help him celebrate the end of examinations. As ill luck for him would have it, there was something in his makeup which produced a total reaction. We got him into a small room and in the 90 minutes before a doctor actually came, I had most of the Sixth Form two at a time in there with him to hold him down and prevent him harming himself. It was a very salutary shock for them all and when the next day the school doctor told the whole school that without taking any more drugs the poor chap could have further attacks without any warning at any time over the next few years, the lesson was clear to all the boys and certainly I did not have any major problems during the next years, though I would be pretty certain that some boys encountered and used drugs at parties when home in the holidays.

Meanwhile, we went on enforcing rules about smoking and drinking. I had a rule that if a boy was caught smoking the severity of the punishment depended upon where he was caught. If it was in the school buildings then there was always the added danger of a fire being caused and this drew a major punishment. If he had taken the trouble to go some distance from the school then the punishment (which was in the first instance a fine – the money to go to Cancer Research) would be determined by the number of fields' distance from the College the miscreant had travelled. A persistent smoker would necessitate the summoning of parents to the College and in their presence an ultimatum that the next offence would merit expulsion.

I enjoyed the vast majority of my time as a Headmaster enormously and there were very few things that I really did not enjoy doing but amongst these, the three most difficult were breaking the news to a pupil that a close relative had died or been killed, getting rid of an unsatisfactory member of staff and expelling a pupil. The first of these is obviously self-explanatory. To dismiss a master meant not only putting his future in jeopardy but also in the case of a married man, undermining the future of his whole family. And yet it had to be done on certain occasions and how does one prove incompetence? 'But Headmaster, you always give me the bottom sets in my subject and the boys are incapable of learning.' Getting rid of a member of staff or a pupil does not end as he walks out of the study. One spends an immense amount of time trying to find employment for the member of staff, or another school who will give the pupil a second chance. Fortunately most Headmasters I found were prepared to take the latter course of action after an interview with the boy and his parents. Indeed I took this line myself but would say to the boy when he came to my study, 'I know why you have left your school and if you come here your Housemaster will know the reason also, but we will be the only ones to know and it will be in your own interests not to broadcast the information yourself. I am prepared to take you into my school but you must realize that any infringement of the rules or anti-social behaviour here will mean that I shall also ask you to leave and you would be most unlikely to find anyone prepared to give you a third chance'. In point of fact, over my years as a Headmaster I suppose I took on a dozen pupils in these circumstances and in all but two cases it was a very successful move. In those two the boys also left Hurstpierpoint!

One of the most difficult aspects of running a school for me during my first years at Hurstpierpoint was finance. Canon Howard had produced a forward-looking development plan but there was very little money in the College funds. The Appeal was proceeding very slowly and inflation was on the increase (it reached 25% in 1975-6). For some years the fees had been kept very low. When I went to Lancing as a boy in 1945 the fees were £50 per term. When I went to Hurstpierpoint as Headmaster in 1964 the fees were £150 per term.

I realized that we were now in an age when society looked with some doubts at a school whose fees were very low on the assumption that it meant that the facilities, the education or even perhaps the catering was 'done on the cheap'. However, one cannot make an immediate and large rise in fees for current parents could not, and probably would not, take it. Nevertheless over these first years the fees did rise so that, as Peter King points out in his history of the College, *The School by the Downs 1849-1995*, the income rose from £185,758 in 1964 to £1,082,970 in 1979 despite which there was never enough money to do what we wanted and what was, in fact, needed. I remember going into the Masters' Common Room after a Governors' meeting in a considerable state of worry and depression as the Governors had just raised the fees to £1,000 per term. Robert Bury saw me looking worried and asked what was the matter. I replied 'the fees are going up to £1,000 a term and I fear that this may mean the end of the College.' His reply was: 'I shouldn't worry, Headmaster, I remember when your predecessor came in here and said the same thing when the fees went up to £100, and we are all still here.'

Indeed the numbers in the school did rise, which did in part help the income, but on the other hand this increase merely meant that there was an increasing need for more buildings and more staff. There was a corresponding increase in the number of ancillary staff needed also. We certainly struggled in these years despite which a number of buildings were put up and others improved. The kitchens at least had been completely renovated. At the beginning of September 1968 the Bursar came to my study with the news that most of our resident work force (kitchen and cleaning staff) had left. They had all had work in Brighton and the area during the summer holidays and found the pay and conditions better. We took an immediate decision to take on a contract cleaning firm and also contract caterers. The cleaning bill rose as expected, the food was expertly managed and did not mean a great increase in costs. Very shortly after we had taken on Gardner Merchant, a senior member of the firm suggested that we might care to install their new range of deep frozen foods which meant provision of a deep freeze room but a great increase in the range of choices. We did this and with great success. Indeed, often potential customers came to visit our kitchen set-up over the next few years which meant from our point of view that high standards had to be maintained. We were fortunate that a senior manager of the firm had come in as our Catering Manager and he was excellent. He also trained up his assistant who took over when he retired and completed 25 very happy and successful years as Catering Manager before he also retired.

We set up a kitchen committee with boy representatives who were thus able to have a direct say in what was provided, which was also good for general morale. There was no doubt though that what the catering staff really enjoyed was putting on an extra such as the Old Boys' Dinner or farewell dinners for leaving staff. They always rose to the occasion and produced something memorable. The Old Boys' Dinner had previously been held annually in London but I suggested to their committee that they might like to hold it back at the College and this was warmly accepted. Numbers attending increased over the years and it has now become an Old Boys' weekend in October with the Dinner on the Saturday evening, following an Evensong in Chapel at which a choir of Old Boys sings the service with the Sunday being the traditional Old Boys' Day – a Eucharist with banner procession for the Feast of St Etheldreda, on whose day the chapel had been dedicated in 1868, followed by an AGM, drinks in the Common room, lunch in Hall and matches (rugby, hockey and sometimes tennis) against the school in the afternoon. A good range of former pupils attends this annual gathering which has now become a fully established part of the calendar.

At my first Etheldreda at the College, I had been invited to speak to those assembled at their AGM about the Appeal. With enthusiasm I was outlining the plans devised mainly by Canon Howard for renovating the older boarding houses and the central block of the College. To my horror, a senior Old Boy rose to his feet: 'Headmaster, Shield House sixty years ago was good enough for me – and it still is today. If you change anything in that building you will never receive a penny from me and I shall see to it that my contemporaries take the same attitude.' At the end of the meeting I had a rare flash of intelligence. I went up to him and said: 'I am afraid that I don't know your name but you clearly have the best interests of the College at heart. I wonder whether I could persuade you to join the Appeal Committee?' He did and not only went on to make a handsome contribution himself to the fund but ensured that his contemporaries did also!

The Appeal did not quite reach its modest target of £64,000 despite meetings held around the country and at the College but there was just sufficient to complete the kitchen development (£59,000). In 1971 we decided to launch another appeal but this time it was to be conducted by ourselves. Frank Florey was given a sabbatical term from his duties to organize it and with the help of senior colleagues we raised eventually by 1976 a total of £109,957. In the course of it I myself wrote over 2,000 letters – in longhand – asking for support or thanking personally everyone who had contributed. But it was not until the mid 1970s that we were able to undertake any major building developments.

There was certainly no possibility of building another boarding house, so in 1972 the Governors took the major decision to build a new Headmaster's House to the north of the College, the other side of the main cricket field. This meant that the Library could be moved from its position as the ground floor of the south west wing, freeing that for Red Cross House, who had been scattered around the building. It meant also that the Housemaster of Star House could now actually have living quarters adjacent to his House (the first floor of the old Headmaster's House). Originally, of course, the Headmaster had also been Housemaster of Star House for which dubious privilege (and the fact that every boy in this House had his own individual washbasin!) they paid an extra £5 per pupil per term. But Canon Howard had wisely decided that you cannot combine headmastering with housemastering and had put in a Housemaster for Star (with a £5 reduction in the fees for boys in that house!)

The results of this scheme were varied. Certainly Red Cross and Star too were better off but the Library was not so satisfactory. From our point of view we had a garden and appropriate privacy but a modern Colt designed house was in no way comparable to the elegant and spacious rooms of the building we had occupied in the centre of the school. Nevertheless we were comfortable and had the fun of creating a garden out of what had been the school's rubbish dump – with appropriate extraordinary finds over the years when digging in the garden.

Chapter 12

IN 1972 THE GOVERNORS gave me a sabbatical term. By this time we had acquired another daughter so with three young children it was difficult to envisage any major move anywhere. Nobly, Diana offered to stay at Hurst whilst I went over to the USA to visit old friends. I was to travel on the great French liner the *SS France*. She had been on an 80 day round the world cruise and this was to be the last eight days of her voyage. I went by train to the South of France and joined the ship at Cannes. We went out to her in small boats and she was a memorable sight, all lit up in a blaze of lights. We first went to Madeira for a day ashore there and then on and gradually arrived in New York.

It was an extraordinary journey. Over half the passengers had disembarked in Europe and we were some 700 passengers with 1,500 crew to look after us. The passengers were mostly Americans returning home and for the first time I had close contact with how much money some of them possess. A very pleasant lady at my table said to me as we neared New York: 'I am worried about what I should tip my cabin steward. You see I have 25 cabin trunks. At each country where we have stopped on this voyage, I have bought two complete national costumes (one male, one female) as I am going to throw a big fancy dress party for my friends when I get home.' She then named a sum of money as a tip, which was more than the cost of my all-inclusive ticket for the eight days' voyage!

An amusing tale from this trip was as follows: I had, in the course of the journey, during which the ship was one class and we could go anywhere, struck up a friendship with the splendid French barman in the First class bar. A day out from New York he asked me whether I would be travelling back to Europe on the

France. I replied, yes, but that I would not be able to see him as I would be travelling Economy class and thus forbidden the First class lounge. 'Monsieur, do not worry' he said, 'there is a way which you can come through. After you have dined down there put on your dinner jacket and go to the ship's Chapel. That is always open for all passengers. Say a little prayer for me as you come through and I will have a gin and tonic waiting for you.' He was quite right and for four nights on the return crossing I did just that – which perhaps proves the value of being a fluent French speaker for very few of the passengers on my outward journey were that, which is why it was appreciated by the crew.

On my arrival in New York I made my way to Pomfret School and spent a very pleasant week there. Five of my former colleagues had now become Headmasters and I was to visit them over the next few weeks but there were still plenty of people I knew. The biggest difference was in the pupils. The blazers, white shirts and school ties had disappeared. Casual gear and casual attitudes prevailed but the students were nevertheless as friendly as ever. Dave Twichell, the Headmaster, asked what my plans were. I told him that I was planning to spend five weeks travelling around the States on the Greyhound buses. With his secretary he worked out that in most of the places I planned to visit there were either former pupils or current parents and presented me with a list of names and telephone numbers so that only four nights in the five weeks was I in a hotel room. Otherwise I was in American homes which was the best possible way to visit the country. I received so much kindness and hospitality. I went from Boston to Chicago via Niagara Falls, then right across the Midwest (Indianapolis) to Denver. There on Dave's advice I took the train over the Rockies to Salt Lake City. That was a memorable journey after days in a bus crossing immense (and dull) plains. The train consisted of only five coaches but one could often see the end of it, so winding was the climb. When we reached the top, we stopped for half an hour. I got out and it was very cold! I had forgotten that the train carriages were all air-conditioned. It really was striking scenery.

In one town in the mid-West my hosts announced that they had arranged for me to be interviewed on the local Radio and TV station about my school in England. Fortunately I had one or two photographs with me and so set off for the studio. There were various other interviews before me. The one immediately before me was a large, obviously country lady in an enormous fur coat. The interviewer was pressing her about this for she had spun it herself entirely out of fur combed from her dogs. He asked if there had been any problems and in a wonderful mid-Western drawl she replied: 'Nope, it's just fine. The only problem is when it's raining; for if it gets wet all the dogs for miles around they just follows me everywhere.' The studio was in a chaos of laughter and I think that the following words on an English boys independent school fell a little flat.

In Salt Lake City I got a hotel room and went down to the lobby. I asked the doorman where the bar was? He replied: 'Sir, you must be a stranger. This city is dry, but' (on seeing the look on my face) 'go down the street, turn first left and at number 20 go down to the basement, knock and say that Sam sent you.' I felt like someone in a B movie but did as was suggested and was let into a small over-crowded bar where a large gin and tonic was soon produced – it was an extraordinary experience.

Then it was on by coach to San Francisco which I think is one of the most exciting cities in the world, Los Angeles which was so traffic-ridden I left hastily and then on to Las Vegas. After finding a hotel I went into one of the large casinos. To my amazement there were even one-armed bandits by each stall in the men's loo! I changed a note for some one dollar coins and in the space of half an hour won two jackpots, which not only paid my hotel bill for the night but also paid for an enormous meal and a visit to the theatre and meant that I left the next morning with more money than when I arrived. I think I am one of the few who could say that!

It is a rather frightening experience to see people sitting for hours feeding money into a one-armed bandit with no expression on their faces and then losing any money that they win and also to be approached by people in the street trying to sell you their wrist watch or wallet (empty) in order to gain some money to go back inside and lose that also. I was glad to have been there and glad to get away.

The Grand Canyon was as awe-inspiring as one is led to believe, Houston was dramatic, New Orleans charmingly French, Charleston beautifully old Colonial and Washington inspiring, though rather grim in that I was warned by my hosts only to walk in certain areas and I believe that it is even more dangerous these days.

I finally arrived back in New York and made my way to South Kent School to stay with my very dear friends George and Maggie Bartlett. George had succeeded his father Sam as Headmaster and it was a truly remarkable school. Everything was done by the pupils – clearing away at meals, cleaning the school, sweeping and weeding the grounds, collecting mail from the village and so on – and it was a happy family community. It was essentially a small school and the Chapel played a very large part in the life of it, which greatly appealed to me. I spent a few happy days there and then it was back to New York and the *France* and back to England. When I arrived at Southampton it was a joy to see Diana and the girls waiting on the quayside. I then learnt that whilst I had been enjoying myself cavorting around the New World, Diana had had a miserable time confined to the house for most of the time as the girls had contracted scarlet fever. They were now fortunately all better and we returned to the school.

Ken Mason had been acting Head in my absence and of course everything had run smoothly. A year later he retired and brought to an end a long and distinguished career at Hurst. He had taught history with great success and had numerous pupils who had gone on to do well at university. He was succeeded as Second Master by Robert Bury, who had also been at the College since 1933, though he had been away during the War on active service. He was another remarkable figure who made a great contribution to Hurst, as Head of Classics, Master-in-Charge of cricket, and as I have mentioned earlier, producer of 28 school Shakespeare plays. For me, one of his most demanding tasks was producing the school timetable each year.

When I first arrived as Headmaster, I was determined to do some teaching and having spent seven years as Sixth Form French master at Charterhouse, wanted to continue with Sixth Form work. Christopher Dean, the Head of Modern Languages, kindly agreed to this but within a couple of years I realized that I did not have the time to keep up with current trends and ideas on French literature. Also the best way to know one's school is to teach the young when they arrive, so I asked to be given junior classes and one Fifth Form set. With these it was possible occasionally to miss a lesson if I had an urgent meeting elsewhere and also over the years it meant that at some time or other I had taught most of the boys in the College. Christopher gave me the bottom French O level set (presumably for the good of my soul) and perhaps unfairly I would greet them at the start of the academic year with the words 'Now you have all got to pass this O level next summer. It is for my sake because if you fail, then everyone can say "The Headmaster just can't teach!"' It may have been unfair, but they certainly worked and there is in my opinion no greater satisfaction in teaching than to lead a very weak candidate to a position where he manages to gain a pass at O level.

Life proceeded very happily in the seventies. I became a magistrate in 1976 and sat on the Mid-Sussex Bench at Haywards Heath and East Grinstead. I found this a most interesting occupation, though at times upsetting, notably in the Juvenile Court. I can still remember to this day one case. We had a 9 year old on a charge of stealing. Both parents were present, each now with a different partner. 'Well, I don't want the little . . .' said the father and the mother said the same. I looked at the boy whose legs did not even reach the ground from the chair on which he was sitting. A tear rolled down his cheek. When we retired to consider a verdict I said to my two fellow magistrates, 'I would like to put both those parents inside for what they have done to that child.' My colleagues, both senior to me, calmed me down and eventually we took the child into care.

On another occasion I was sitting in the Crown court at Lewes. The accused, who had a record which went from probation to juvenile detention centre, to prison on several occasions, was accused of robbing and assaulting an old lady on the seafront at Hastings. I had been warned by fellow magistrates that the Judge with whom I was sitting was known to the criminal fraternity as Father Christmas. When we retired to consider our verdict, we talked for some 20 minutes and he then said, 'Well, I think this is a case for probation. What do you think?' 'My Lord,' I replied, 'I was thinking of at least 3 years inside'. The Judge turned to my fellow magistrate: 'Well I think 5 years.' After considerable discussion the Judge conceded that it was two to one and agreed on a prison sentence. We went back into court and he said, 'My colleagues and I have considered this very carefully and you will go to prison for 3 years.'

There was an immediate outcry and commotion in the courts as the defendant's family (he was a gipsy and they were there in force) shouted and banged the floor. The Judge cleared the court and it was the end of the morning. As I approached the main entrance of Lewes Crown Court to go out, the police sergeant on the door held me back. 'Excuse me Sir, but you were sitting on that last case weren't you?' 'Yes I was indeed.' 'Well, Sir, I wouldn't go out that way if I were you. The defendant's family are beating up his solicitor as he had assured them that with that Judge sitting he was likely to get off with at worst probation. I will let you out by the back door, Sir.' I slunk to my car and drove hastily back to Hurst.

The Chairman of the Bench, Mrs Joan Kleinwort, was a lovely person. She lived in a beautiful house near Haywards Heath, called Heaselands, to which we were invited on several occasions. She also very generously invited us on several memorable evenings to Glyndebourne, where she had the Glyndebourne box to herself and visitors as her husband was a sponsor of the opera company. Glyndebourne was, in those days, the mecca of opera going as far as I was concerned, though we did pay occasional visits to Covent Garden and the ENO until sadly productions at the latter opera house tended to become modern interpretations of old established favourites which spoilt them for me.

As well as sitting on the bench, I had also become involved with the British Overseas Trade Board on whose language committee I sat, and also with the English Speaking Union Education Committee. I was also governing three prep schools and sat on the Governing Body of Bishop Otter College in Chichester. Despite all these commitments I still found time to teach nearly a half timetable and also to produce the occasional play and act in Common Room extravaganzas. There was also still the primary task of 'selling the school'. Apart from visiting preparatory schools and entertaining their Heads, I made a point of not just seeing but also personally showing round every prospective parent who came to Hurst. This took a great deal of time but most certainly paid off because I reckon that about 80% of those who came actually entered their son for the College. It was also a very useful way of seeing that all was well in and around the school as I walked the visitors around.

I remember one occasion when, as we passed the changing rooms of one House, a volley of bad language came out. I apologized to the visitors and at the next school assembly I referred to this incident, said how embarrassed I had been and how that in my opinion using bad language was merely a sign of a weak intellect. A couple of days later, I was in my study with my Golden Retriever, Nimrod, and eldest daughter, Elizabeth aged, I suppose 3 or 4. There was a knock at the door and as it opened, Nimrod rushed out at which Elizabeth cried 'Come here you bloody dog'! Five minutes later, there was another knock at the door and the mischievous face of the Head Boy appeared. 'Weak intellect, Sir?' he queried to which there was no reply.

I know that many Headmasters use senior pupils to show parents around, but I never took that step. I think that on the whole boys, however difficult they may be, will, however, always give of their best for the school, though having said that I am reminded of the parent I was showing round who remarked: 'It is good of you to show us around, Headmaster. What is your attitude towards games?' To which my reply was, 'I am no games player whatsoever myself but for those who wish to play there is a wide choice and they are given every encouragement. If they are like me then they will play perhaps twice a week with boys of a similar inclination and a master-in-charge who is not a fanatic. I still think it is good for them to learn and acquire a certain sense of team spirit.' The visitors replied: 'Thank you. I asked because recently we visited . . . . . . (he named another rival school in the area) and were shown around by a pupil whose reply to my question was: 'If your son is keen on games don't send him here. We never win at anything'. So the use of pupils is not always a guarantee of success with prospective parents.

I made it a rule never to show more than three sets of parents round in any one day, as it is both time-consuming and tiring. On one occasion, my secretary had, for once, blundered and I had a fourth set. On our way round, I launched into my spiel: 'We went over to cafeteria feeding a few years ago and the boys like it. It means they can sit where they like and also get a choice of menu.' 'I presume, Headmaster, you mean red or white wine', said the husband and to my horror we were standing in the Chapel, not the Dining Hall, and I had begun a 'mechanical' tour of the school. I apologized and we laughed and their son was entered for Hurst, so I suppose that all was well in the end.

The years passed by so quickly. The three girls went to school locally at first, then Elizabeth and Helen went to the PNEU school for Girls in Burgess Hill and Caroline to a prep school, Handcross Park. We had decided that they should all try to get into St Swithun's School at Winchester, mainly because our old friend, Olwen Davies, who had been a Headmistress in Brighton, was now Headmistress there. Elizabeth and Helen both passed in at ages 13 and 11 and began there. It also began a series of many trips on the A272, an attractive but essentially winding, country road for Diana on whom the burden of travel fell, because I always seemed to have commitments at school. Caroline also sat the Common Entrance at the age of eleven and joined her sisters at St Swithun's. Sadly, it was not a good move. It is sometimes a failure on the part of school teachers to criticize a pupil by comparing progress with that of another member of the family and she was often compared unfavourably with her sisters. This gave her, totally unjustly, a tremendous lack of self-confidence. Her progress and career since she left school have proved that she is decidedly not unintelligent and that she has a practical sense of what is right and wrong and of how to deal with other people that have marked her out as a very special person and one who is much liked and respected.

But it became clear that whilst Elizabeth was a born rebel but one who made a full contribution to school life both in the sporting world and musically and Helen went on to be Head Girl, Caroline was not happy but she was determined to stay the course and so became a weekly boarder until leaving after taking her O levels.

Diana had acquired a horse and there were ponies for the girls, though Caroline was the one who showed the most promise and interest. Part of a far corner of the playing fields, which was never used for sport, was fenced off and we built a small stable block at

The family about 1974.

the house. These animals were a source of joy to the family though I must confess I was always a little wary. Then – for me – a disastrous day occurred. We had in the school a boy who was very keen on sport but during one holiday had a disastrous accident which left him paralysed from the waist down. He went to Stoke Mandeville Hospital and after about six months I received a letter from the senior doctor there to ask whether we could consider having him back in the school despite the fact that he was permanently confined to a wheelchair. Our remarkable San. sister, Winifred Berry, agreed to have him permanently resident in the school Sanatorium and so he came back. We put ramps in various places around the school and otherwise boys would carry him + wheelchair up and down staircases to the dining hall and classroom block. Sister Berry gradually urged him into propelling himself short distances on arm crutches until the day when she announced to me that he would walk from the Sanatorium to our house unaided (apart from crutches) on the understanding that if he was successful I would ride Diana's horse from our house to the San!

On the given afternoon virtually the whole school lined the road to cheer him on. It was about 300 yards and took him the best part of two hours but he did it and so, in a state of panic, I was helped onto this horse and with someone leading it made the (to me) perilous journey back through a cheering school. The only time in my life that I have been on a horse. The boy did well and having won a Douglas Bader Scholarship ended up as a Flight Controller at Gatwick Airport, so we could claim a real success for Hurst.

So many things happened during those years. I had decided that we would only have an official Prize Day with guest speaker once every four years – to enable me to choose really distinguished speakers and to ensure that the boys and their parents had one memorable day to remember from their time in the College. The other years we would have an Open Day instead with the College on show at work and at play, with societies and activities setting up displays for the visitors. At one stage in the afternoon I would speak to the parents in the theatre. Despite the fact that this was advertised, when I walked into the theatre at 3.00 p.m. there were only two parents there so we retired to my study and had an informal chat for half an hour. Things were better in succeeding years! I did find throughout my time that parents were, with a very few exceptions, extremely co-operative and enthusiastic about what went on in the place. The first guest speaker I had was Sir Robert Birley, at that stage retired from the Headmastership of Eton and currently a professor at the City University in London. He lumbered onto the stage with me and I could sense the audience, boys and parents, wondering who on earth this was. His opening words caught their imagination and held them for an inspiring twenty minutes. 'When I was at school, one term I came top of my form in the examinations. When the report arrived on the breakfast table I sat in an agony of expectancy as my father read it in the hope that this might be worth at least a fiver. My father read it in silence, then handed it over to me. My Housemaster had written: "Birley, first. But the others were worse." Later that day parents were asking me for copies of his speech. Sadly we had not recorded it and so far as I could see from where I was sitting it consisted of half a dozen words on the back of an envelope!

Four years later we listened to Sir David Hunt, who had just won the BBC Mastermind programme, another eminently gifted speaker and then four years from that we had Lord Denning. He came thanks to my next Chairman of Governors, Sir Desmond Heap, Comptroller of the City of London and City Solicitor and currently President of the Law Society. I remember that speech particularly for Lord Denning's opening words. Desmond had given him a very flowery and impressive introduction. Lord Denning began in his wonderful Hampshire burr, 'Sir Desmond's speech reminds me of the sign over the chemist's shop in my little village in Hampshire which reads, "We dispense with accuracy".' Another memorable speech followed by the official opening of the first major building project I had achieved – a magnificent new Music School in the design of which we had been given much useful advice by one of the Governors, John Birch, then Organist and Master of the Choristers at Chichester Cathedral but shortly to go to take over the music at the Temple Church in London.

It never ceases to amaze me that the standard of music at the College had been so high during those early years. There was only a hut out on the North Field which held a few pianos in practice rooms and visiting teachers had to make do with odd venues around the buildings, including the Chapel vestry and the Director of Music's sitting room, despite which we had concerts of a high standard and a choir capable of singing magnificent services, together with a major choral work each year with chorus and augmented school orchestra. A succession of gifted music masters went back to Horace Hawkins, who was there from 1915-1938 before he moved to Chichester Cathedral and who had taken the choir to Paris in 1931 where they had met his old teacher, C.M. Widor, who composed a piece of music for them and which is still performed in Chapel. By the 1980s, the College had acquired a musical reputation nationally. In 1977 the choir had performed in the Schools Music Association concert at the Royal Festival Hall and in 1983 they won the National Schools Choir Competition. There had also been LP recordings and in general the music was of a very high standard, which continues to the present day.

The dramatic scene had also developed. From just one school play a year (Shakespeare), the theatre was now in constant use with a succession of school plays, including Kafka's *The Trial* (1965), Anouilh's *Ring Around the Moon* (1971), Eliot's *Murder in the Cathedral* (1973) and Pinter's *The Birthday Party* (1982). There were house plays and the Junior School was also encouraged to put on stage productions. We also had the Common Room Gilbert and Sullivan productions mentioned already.

Societies were flourishing also with many activities involved (in one term in the mid-seventies, there were 200 meetings in one Michaelmas Term) and there were societies to carry on from classroom subjects such as carpentry, computing, pottery, silver smithing etc. I was pleased at the number of masters and boys involved for in the first years of my time at the College there had been a distinct lack of interest and enthusiasm for extra-curricular activities.

The years continued to race past and 1981 saw my fiftieth term at Hurst – and the Governors kindly gave it to me as a sabbatical. This time, with all three girls away at boarding school, I was able to spend some of it with Diana, unlike 1972 when the girls had been so much smaller. We drove first to the north and then came back down the eastern side of the country visiting Cathedrals and Abbeys as we moved south, arriving back in time to see the girls over half-term. We then crossed over the channel and drove through to Vienna, which was as magical as I had always imagined. We went to the Spanish Riding School and to the Schönbrunn Palace, heard the Vienna Boys Choir sing a Sunday Mass and spent an evening at the Volksoper – *The Merry Widow*. The memory of the latter was of the whole audience, mostly in evening dress, swaying in time to the music and quietly singing along with the words. Another vivid memory was walking back to our hotel at midnight through silent, dark streets but with not the slightest worry or fear about muggings etc. – and there are not many towns where one can do that let alone cities!

We were back in time for the end of term Carol Services. George Lambert, who had been acting Headmaster, greeted me with relief. He said. 'I have been here since 1937, apart from the War, and you are the fourth Headmaster under whom I have served, but I had no idea of how many and varied are the problems with which you have to deal every day of the term. I hope you don't mind, but I have taken the liberty of telling the members of the Common Room that in future they should bring problems to me and I will sort them out and deal with all the minor issues, leaving only the big ones to you.' What a man! And what a great help to a Headmaster. Life continued as busy as ever, nevertheless with teaching commitments, committees, Governing Body meetings in the various schools I had been asked to help with and all the petty details of school life which still came my way.

Yet I would not have changed it for anything in the world. I think that I have been extremely fortunate in my whole life. Lancing had been a joy and so had King's College Cambridge. I had then had the brief time at New College and Westminster School, a wonderful period in France and then Charterhouse with the year in the USA as an added bonus. And now I had 50 terms behind me and was still only 50 years old. There had been problems, of course, and I had managed to survive these. But I began to wonder whether it was good for Hurstpierpoint and indeed for me and my family to continue. There were plenty of criticisms that the place was run in a very old-fashioned and autocratic way though I myself think that I did encourage discussion and debate and also change in the general running of affairs.

One of the first things I did on my appointment to Hurst was to acquire a dog. There had always been dogs at my parents' home and we had grown up with them. It had not been possible to have a dog at Charterhouse but now in my second term in Sussex I brought a splendid Golden Retriever named (in honour of my favourite composer) Nimrod. He was a great character and like all of that breed a lover of people, so he was a great success in the school. I had one disaster with him, however. I decided to take him into class with me one day as an aid to French oral discussion. I attached his lead to the master's desk and then began my usual habit of wandering around the classroom whilst teaching. What I had not reckoned on was Nimrod following me around the room! The first intimation of this was a crash as the desk overturned and its contents, meticulously arranged by the owner, Ken Mason, the Second Master, were spread all over the floor. This was a great delight to the class but Nimrod's only appearance in a classroom!

In due course of time at the age of nearly 10, he died and we bought another Golden Retriever, Brandy, who kept up the tradition of popularity with the boys. During his long life we had tried various other breeds as companions to him but without any lasting success. One day after a family discussion on how to replace him when he died, one of the girls spotted an advertisement in the Times offering St. Bernard puppies for sale. There was an immediate response from Diana and indeed all the girls, but I firmly rejected it. Their disappointment was so great that I took myself off to the study and rang the kennels. 'Do you want a dog for show purposes or as a family pet?' I replied the latter and was told that there was just one left, the runt of the litter and not perfectly marked. When I returned home I told the family that the following day I was to drive to a village near Cambridge to see this puppy!

Diana and I parked the car in the car park of the village pub. On the back seat of the car next to us was a bundle of fur. Of course, we both fell for it. As I handed over the cheque, I said to the breeder,

'You said this was the runt. How large will he grow?' 'About 16-18 stone' came the reply and on seeing my horrified gaze she added, 'His brothers will end up well over 20 stone.'

As a puppy (see picture on page 142) his diet seemed enormous but as he grew he ate less and eventually consumed not much more than a large Golden Retriever, but his eventual size was 17 stone. We knew this because on one occasion when he was ill and the vet needed to know his weight for prescription purposes, Diana drove to the local weighbridge for vehicles and got on the machine with Bumble, as we called him, and then deducted her own weight from the total.

He was amicability itself and much loved by the family and the school. He moved slowly and thought slowly – the one hazard was if someone called him over. He would slowly get up a good turn of speed but then found it difficult to stop and over the years bowled over a number of those who had called him to them! When we moved to our cottage his size dominated the place but he remained a dear member of the family for nine years when his kidneys packed up. He was much missed, leaving a big hole in our lives. Two Labrador puppies, one black, one yellow, litter brothers, came to be with us after Bumble died and gave us infinite devotion for nine and a half and thirteen years and proved to us to be the best of all family dogs.

I had put in for the Headship of other schools – initially Repton, though I knew on visiting there that I was not the right person for it, Stowe and although that would have been a real challenge, my Woodard background ruled me out as far as the Governors there were concerned and Lancing, though I am not sure it would have been wise to go back to my old school and to a place I knew well from our Southern Division connections. The disappointment that I was unsuccessful in my applications was completely overruled by my happiness at remaining at Hurst. Financially the College was in a much sounder state and as well as much restoration of the older houses, we were able to undertake some major new building works. The most ambitious of these was to build a new Science building. The existing one had been put up in 1950 and had become far too small and limited over the years. An elegant new building was put up where the old Tuckshop had stood (the latter had been moved to the East (rugby) field as changing rooms) and in 1985 the Duke of Edinburgh flew in by helicopter to open it. It was named in honour of one Governor, Sir Frank Mason, the distinguished Engineer in Chief of the Fleet, who for some years had been Chairman of Prince Philip's committee on School Technology. The royal visit was a memorable day for Hurst and the royal visitor was scrupulous in making sure that he spoke to every boy working in every room he visited. To my initial worry, until I realized that I could rely on my boys, as I presented the school prefects to him, he motioned to me to go away and as I left, I heard him say, 'Now, I want to hear the real low-down on this place!'

In 1984 I had learnt that Malvern College was to become vacant. It was a school that I had much admired and after consultation with friends I put in for it. I had a whole day visit from a Malvern Governor and his wife to see how I got on in my own school and then an interview board in London, which I thought went extremely well. But it was not to be and so at the age of 53 I began to think in terms of seven more years at Hurstpierpoint.

One morning the telephone rang in my office. It was my very good friend Ian Beer, who had left Lancing and was now at Harrow. 'Roger, you have been at Hurst quite long enough. Why don't you put in for the post of Secretary of HMC?' I had seen this advertised some months before but had never thought of applying. After some further conversation, I put the phone down. About half an hour later it went again. Another great friend, John Thorn, Headmaster of Winchester, who addressed me in exactly the same words as Ian. (I learnt later that the Committee had rejected the applications they had received and the Chairman had asked individual members to approach anyone they thought might do the job). I talked it over with Diana and then went to London to see

The opening of the Frank Mason Science Laboratories, May 1985.

the current Secretary, Robson Fisher, who had been Chief Master of King Edward's Birmingham. What I heard appealed to me and after consultation with my Chairman of Governors, Sir John Barnes, I sent off my application.

I was summoned to interview in London at the HMC office in Islington. The selection committee consisted of three great friends from HMC, Bruce McGowan, Headmaster of Haberdashers' Aske's, David Emms from Dulwich but whom I had known when he was at Cranleigh and Christopher Everett, Headmaster of Tonbridge, and three people who had never met me, Peter Snape, the General Secretary of the Secondary Heads Association, Derek Dutton, President of SHA and Florence Kirkby, a formidable former Headmistress and SHA expert on pensions. It was an extraordinary interview in that I knew three of them so well and three not at all. I answered a number of questions on a variety of subjects but felt that I had not presented myself very well. As I left the building, I caught a glimpse of a very well-known member of HMC going in and realized that if he were another candidate then my chances of success were indeed slight.

I got home in somewhat of a gloom and was treating myself to a large gin and tonic when the phone rang. It was Bruce McGowan to offer me the post. I was delighted to accept it on the spot.

Chapter 13

AT THAT TIME HMC did not have its own Secretariat. I was appointed as Deputy Secretary of SHA, with special responsibility for HMC members. This, of course, was why half the members of the selection committee had been from that organization. Robson Fisher had been due to retire at Christmas 1985 but agreed to stay on until April so that Hurstpierpoint had more time to appoint my successor and so that I had time to arrange my affairs.

It was a shock to realize that after nearly 22 years in the same place I was to move. In the Spring of 1985 Diana and I had found a small cottage in the village of Cocking, just south of Midhurst in the very west of West Sussex. We had been looking for a holiday home for a couple of years and had found that we could not afford the ones we really liked and then suddenly there arrived in the morning post details of Hanbury Cottage which appealed. We had driven over (one hour from Hurstpierpoint) in snow and looked around it. It clearly needed much doing to it but we thought we had plenty of time during the next seven years until I retired. I contacted a parent who was a surveyor and he very kindly went over and inspected the cottage. His report was that much needed doing but if we liked it he would recommend it as a sound investment but we must re-wire and re-roof before moving in. We put in a bid and the whole business was concluded in six weeks, which must be near a record.

The cottage had appealed to both of us immediately we saw it. I think we both saw the potential there and it is in a lovely part of West Sussex. And it has certainly lived up to all our expectations. When the three girls first saw it they immediately expressed the view that their parents were mad – now each one of them would like to live in it as it has become a real family home. I just wish that it was a little bigger for family gatherings which stretch our resources to the full.

There were a few essentials that needed immediate attention. There was no damp course and no central heating. Also there was a hole in the roof and numerous tiles were loose or broken. We found a local builder who dealt with all these details and then we thought we were nicely settled. Now, however, we had a few months during which we must turn a small holiday cottage into a family home. The first major move was to get planning permission to turn a tumbledown garage and former laundry room into a dining room and utility room. It is Grade II listed but we obtained the permission. When the garage was cleared of a mountain of rubbish we found some wonderful old beams, part of which were clearly ships' timbers and which have made an excellent and attractive dining room.

In the old laundry room was the original 'copper' which now occupies a central position in the garden. Apparently some ninety years ago, when there were very few houses in the village, everyone brought their laundry to Hanbury Cottage on a Monday morning! The cottage is very old. We have traced it back in the County Archives to the early sixteenth century but I think that it is earlier than that. It was originally two single-storey cottages with one central fireplace between them. Under the roof are two major cross beams on which the inhabitants clearly stored their farm implements and hay and straw but which, now that there is an upstairs floor, present two major hazards for anyone moving from the two main bedrooms to the bathroom as they are chest high to me when I stand up. I still occasionally hit my head but in the first few months this was almost a daily occurrence and all doorways in the cottage are also a hazard by from 2-4 inches for me and even more for taller visitors!

Our last two terms at Hurstpierpoint were filled with farewell parties and thoughts that this was the last – Carol Service, school play, school concert etc. We were given a most generous send off by everyone and to my greatest astonishment I found that Reg Ruddock, the Second Master, had written to all past and present parents and I was presented with a cheque for over £4,000, which was a great help towards the cottage renovation.

When the last few weeks arrived I began to wonder what I was doing. Hurst had been my life for nearly twenty-two years and I could not really envisage life without it. There began a succession of 'the last . . .' and each one brought home to me how much I would miss it all, especially the people. There was a farewell dinner with the Old Boys, a farewell dinner with the Common room and their wives, my last service in the Chapel and then finally the last calling over – the meeting of the whole school to end the term and which was the real goodbye. It was an emotional time and I was saved from tears in public by a splendid gesture from the Head Boy. He made a little speech which began, 'Headmaster, you once told me that when you were at school you never ever won your House Colours for anything, let alone the School Colours. We have all admired the fact that for nearly twenty-two years you have braved the (sometimes) appalling weather to stand for hours on a touch line or boundary to watch your school play a variety of sports, when you would certainly have been happier at a concert or a play. It has been greatly appreciated by us all and so we have decided to award you your First Team colours for all the major sports.' – at which point six boys, the captains of the various sports, including football, cricket, hockey, squash, athletics and cross-country running, came up to the dais and each gave me the appropriate tie – which I still wear with great pride. It was a wonderfully kind and thoughtful gesture which made the parting seem even more difficult. But we got through it and set about the gigantic task of sorting out and moving the accumulated treasures and junk of twenty-two years.

There was much furniture that we could not take with us. The school bought from me the furniture I had purchased for the Headmaster's Study, which was all on the large side. A major building work we had undertaken was a link building between the main school and the Headmaster's House, built in knapped flint and with pointed neo-Gothic roof so that it fits in well and makes two excellent open quadrangles with the existing buildings. The Headmaster's Study is in the centre on the ground floor with a fine bow window and looking south across the lawns with the South Downs in the distance. Here I left my magnificent partner's desk, the great bookcase my great aunt had given me and a fine table used at Governors' meetings. It is a strange sensation still after fifteen years when I go back into that room. To one side was my secretary's office and to the other a study for the Second Master and on the first and second floors study bedrooms for Sixth Formers.

We managed to take most of the furniture from our house though it meant that the cottage was greatly over-crowded at first. Now that the three girls are married, some of it has disappeared.

I found that I missed the College dreadfully at first but the real shock to the system was having to become a commuter for the first time in my life. At Charterhouse I had walked some 300 yards from my rooms to my classroom, at Hurstpierpoint I had walked some 400 yards from home to my study. Now I had to get up at 7.00 a.m., leave at 7.20 to drive to Haslemere, park the car, fight onto the 7.56 to Waterloo (usually standing most of the journey) join the underground to Oxford Circus, fight onto the Victoria Line to Highbury & Islington and then walk 5 minutes to the office in St Paul's Road. Even worse was the return journey in the evening rush hour, rarely arriving home before 7.15 p.m. I was certainly not cut out for commuting and never learnt to relax when the train was late and no-one explained why or how long we might be.

I had inherited from Robson a secretary who decided to leave

A reluctant commuter returns home, 1987.

after a couple of months but with the salary we were offering I found it well nigh impossible to obtain a good replacement and arrived home one evening having just dismissed her third successor. Before I could say anything Diana said: 'I can't take this any longer, no children at home, no school, no people and I can't do the house and garden all day, every day. I am going to get a job.' My immediate reply was, 'If the committee will wear it, what about coming with me to London as my secretary?', for she had been a secretary before going to Hurst Junior School as Matron. The committee agreed to a trial period and so began for me, and for all the members of HMC, a very happy partnership.

One immediate problem arose. After a couple of months of very unsatisfactory commuting I had decided (despite the very definite drop in my finances since ceasing to be a Headmaster) to invest in a first class season ticket to ensure a seat on the journey to London at the start of each busy day. This was even in 1986 an expensive outlay but worth it. But could we afford two first class season tickets? The answer was no and so – until my daughter, and even more my mother, found out – we would drive together to Haslemere, stand on the platform at different points, join up again at London Waterloo and proceed together to the office! Not a very gentlemanly conduct I freely confess. As soon as my season ticket expired we travelled together in standard class!

It was however, a great joy to have Diana with me, not just for being together but because she was also a most efficient secretary. Everything was done at speed and with accuracy and we prided ourselves that all letters were answered and problems dealt with on the day when they arrived. To my mind her greatest achievement, however, was to get to know and remember all the members of HMC by name, so that particularly at the Annual Conference she could great each arrival personally which made all, and especially new members, feel welcome and at ease. She also managed to remember virtually all the names of members' wives, which was even more appreciated.

The office building in Islington was far too small. It contained the Secretary of SHA, Peter Snape and his secretary, Shirley Chapman, the SHA Assistant Secretary, two receptionists, a lady who administered the paperwork for SHA, Diana and myself and the Secretary of the Girls Schools Association (GSA). It spread over three floors plus a meeting room and storage rooms in the basement. All the rooms were small and Diana operated in the attic. Over the course of the first few months there I discovered that Robson's and at first my secretary's idea of filing was to shove everything under the desk. In this way we uncovered, gradually, letters and dividend cheques going back several years. One of my main tasks was to keep and prepare for annual audit the accounts of HMC, something I had never had to do in my life but which I gradually acquired the knack of doing.

As Deputy Secretary I was required to take the minutes at HMC Committee and at all HMC Sub-Committees. Initially I made far too many notes but gradually acquired the know-how to put down only the essentials. I had only been in Islington about a month when one morning as I arrived Peter Snape greeted me with the words, 'Shirley is ill so you will have to take the minutes at today's SHA Council meeting'. The SHA Council has over 80 members of whom I knew the President, Peter Snape and two others. As the meeting progressed I found myself constantly asking my neighbour, the redoubtable Florence Kirkby, the name of each speaker. After my fourth query she said somewhat frostily, 'You don't know much do you' which silenced me for the rest of the day's proceedings.

I soon realized, however, that what so many members were in need of was a shoulder on which to cry! Indeed some two years on in to the job I was introduced at a meeting by Michael McCrum, then Head Master of Eton, as 'Roger Griffiths the man with the wettest shoulders in HMC.' So often a Headmaster will have a problem but does not know to whom he can turn for advice. One is always a little reluctant to let on to fellow Heads that one has a major worry and yet there are so many times when one needs the experience of another Head to help one out.

I found as the weeks and months went by that what I needed to be was a good listener. So often the telephone would ring and the caller would begin, 'Roger, can you spare five minutes?' Some twenty or thirty minutes later I would say, 'And what have you decided to do?' after which I could say, 'I think that is absolutely the right action to take' or 'I really would not do that for the following reasons . . .' As I became more experienced I could often say, 'Get in touch with the HM of . . . . . . as he had a very similar experience last year and is still successfully in post. I am sure he will help you.' Over the course of 11 years in the post there were very few completely new problems which arose and I always had the vast experience of the General Secretary of SHA and the excellent team of SHA Field Officers to fall back on, which I did on numerous occasions.

These Field Officers were usually retired Heads of great experience who provided a magnificent service for members. On a number of occasions I took a SHA Field Officer with me when I had to deal with a particularly tough problem or difficult governing body, and every time they were of immense help. Another great standby was the Assistant Secretary of AMMA (the Assistant Masters and Mistresses Association) now ATL (the Association of Teachers and Lecturers) David Authers, who was designated to deal with the independent school members. We had over the years many 'non-conversations' which enabled us to solve problems – sometimes caused by his members, sometimes by mine – before they reached crisis point.

There was no doubt that my job was a very personal one and I made it clear to all HMC that I could be contacted at any time of day or night, in the office or at my home, if there was a problem. Over the years I received many telephone calls but usually at a reasonable time of day or night!

This was the real meat of the post for I have never greatly

enjoyed committee meetings and now found myself having to act as Secretary and to take minutes at HMC full Committee (6 times a year), Academic Policy, Professional Development, Membership and Sports Sub-Committees (3 times a year each). Some were very much more interesting than others but the most appealing to me was the Membership Sub-Committee for here we were dealing not only with the problems of individual members (with which I had usually been involved already) but also with applications for membership of HMC.

The latter provided me with some of the most interesting experiences of my life. A school wishing to join had first of all to submit their academic results of the past few years, plus factual information about the size of the school, size of Sixth Form etc. If these met the criteria laid down by the Committee I would then get in touch informally with two or three current members in the same area of the country to ask their opinion of the school and its Head. Following on from that I would set up an inspection team, usually four in number including myself, who would go down to visit the school. One of the team would inspect History and Geography, one would look at Mathematics and the Sciences, one would look at English, the Classics and RI and I would deal with Modern Languages, Art and Music. That was the rough divide and then between us we would look at all the other aspects of the school – boarding facilities, games provision, drama, societies and extra curricular activities and I would deal with the financial situation and the Governing Body.

We would arrive in time for lunch with the Head on the first day and would then be shown around the school by pupils, preferably individually. Heads of Department would have been asked to prepare us a timetable so that over the next 60 hours we could, if possible, visit all the teaching staff in that department and also see all different age groups of pupils. (I let it be known that we might not stay for the duration of a whole lesson but that early departure from a room did not indicate disapproval). We would also see individually the Heads of Department, the Head, the Deputy Head(s), the Bursar, the Chaplain, the Chairman of Governors and, if possible, a senior official of the old pupils' association. We would be staying in a hotel near the school where our own private discussion room was essential. On the first evening we would have an informal buffet supper with all the Common Room and then the second evening we would hope to have dinner with two or three Governors and their spouses and a similar number of senior staff. The last evening we would dine on our own in the hotel and then have a full discussion session on our findings. Lunch each day, apart from the day of arrival, would be taken with the pupils. On the morning of the last (fourth) day we would have a full session alone with the Head in order to make our findings and observations clear and we would leave after lunch. I would then, after receiving written comments from the members of the team, write a full report with recommendations for the Membership Sub-Committee and would present it at their next meeting. Occasionally we would recommend a delay in election of perhaps one or two years during which some of our more trenchant criticisms might be acted upon. At the end of that time if the membership application was renewed, I would pay a day's visit on my own to see what notice had been taken of our suggestions and then report back to the Sub-Committee. This seemed to be a good way of ensuring that the high standards of HMC were maintained and also provided a useful set of information for the Head and Governors.

It is interesting to note that when Government policy turned to ensuring the inspection of all schools, HMC set up its own scheme, approved by the Government agency OFSTED (Office for Standards in Education) which was largely a much extended version of our membership inspection arrangements, which meant that the final document produced for the school was couched in a friendly, informative and personal style which was of considerable help to those there. Now that the inspection of HMC schools has been taken over by OFSTED that aspect has changed considerably and the documents are in an official language which may seem at times bland and which certainly does not offer as much personal assistance to those running the school in question. That is a personal view of course but is to me rather sad.

A number of current Heads of HMC schools, and on occasions if we were looking at a co-educational establishment, Heads of GSA schools, were very active and helpful in this work and over the years a number of excellent establishments joined the ranks of HMC. There were occasional very amusing moments. I remember arriving at Frensham Heights School for an inspection. It is of course a progressive boarding school, and as I got out of the car I was accosted by a large extremely scruffy looking youth who greeted me as follows: 'Hullo Sir, I much prefer it here to being at Hurstpierpoint, there are not nearly so many rules'. It was a boy I had expelled in my last term at Hurstpierpoint for his persistent and flagrant breaching of all rules! And it was a very good introduction to Frensham Heights, which incidentally we elected unanimously and happily into membership.

I have told how in 1972 I had become a Liveryman of the Worshipful Company of Wax Chandlers in the City of London. In 1986 to my great delight I was invited to join the Court of the Company, whose main object was directing the well-being of the Company and dispensing charitable monies which the Company had accrued over the centuries. The Company has its own small but elegant Hall in Gresham Street EC2 (next door to the Goldsmiths) and there the Court would meet six times a year, the meeting followed by a lunch at which Liverymen and guests were also present. The Hall can seat a maximum of 64 for a meal and there was always a good turnout. Also twice a year there were dinners for Liverymen and their partners and once a year a dinner for Masters and Clerks of other Livery Companies at which members of the Court acted as hosts. The big event was in January when after the Court meeting the lunch was attended by the current Lord Mayor and one or both the Sheriffs together with the City Marshal.

Being on the Court meant that I was in London rather more frequently and I got to know the City quite well. One of its finest features is the number and beauty of small Churches that are still active there and I to this day will still look into any I happen to be passing. There are some very remarkable buildings indeed and a great part of our English heritage. The Court consists of 16 members, 8 of whom are past Masters and the remainder of whom will progress in time to becoming Master. Over the next few years two of those senior to me withdrew from the Court for business reasons and so in 1988/89 I found myself Renter Warden, whose main task is to conduct the annual inspection of the building and annual stocktaking of all the Company silver. The following year I became Upper Warden and on August 2nd 1990 I was elected Master of the Worshipful Company of Wax Chandlers.

In past times, there was an election ceremony attended in London by the Court and their ladies and members of the Livery but by 1990 sadly this had disappeared. The Clerk was unwilling for us even to have a small gathering in the Hall and so the actual handing over of the chair of office from my predecessor as Master, Robin Chaventré, took place in the garden at Hanbury Cottage on August 2nd. Robin and his wife Carolyn were staying in the area for Glorious Goodwood and so came over for lunch and we all then went off for a great afternoon at the races. I am glad to say that the ceremony of installation of the Master has now been restored and takes place in London on the first Thursday in August each year.

This was indeed a memorable year for me. In the course of it I was guest at thirty two of the Livery Companies in the City. This meant visiting a variety of Livery Halls each one quite different and all of them elegant, yet warm and welcoming. The ancient ceremonies of Election of the Lord Mayor and Election of the Sheriffs provided an opportunity to walk fully robed in procession

Dinner at the Mansion House, 1991.

with all my fellow Masters and Prime Wardens and on each occasion with the Aldermen of the City to the Guildhall. This happened also at the memorable United Guilds Service and Festival of the Sons of the Clergy at St Paul's Cathedral; the latter attended by the Archbishop of Canterbury as well as the Lord Mayor. Other pieces of City history I attended were the Silent Ceremony when the Lord Mayor took over office from his predecessor, the Trial of the Pyx at the Goldsmiths' Company and the Boars Head Feast at the Cutlers' Company. At the last of these I was reminded of Hurstpierpoint for the first Headmaster, Dr Lowe, had introduced this to the College in the 1850s and it is still celebrated to this day. I was able to present to the Master of the Cutlers' Company the short monograph on the Hurstpierpoint Boars Head feast written by Peter King, Head of History at the College in the 1980s.

The Boar's Head Feast is a ceremony which takes place at the beginning of December. The first Headmaster of Hurstpierpoint, Edward Lowe, had seen it at the Queen's College in Oxford, from which source it had also been adopted by the Cutlers' Company.

At Hurst to this day the choir form up in the cloisters and bearers with lighted torches accompany them. They are preceded by the Head Chef in full chef's regalia who follows a Boar's Head carried aloft by two Sacristans. The whole procession is led by the smallest chorister, named the Lord High Mustard Pot, who carries an enlarged mustard pot on a cushion. The choir process through the cloisters in the darkness lit only by the torches and sing the old song Caput Apri Defero. The ceremony is followed by a special dinner for the choir in the Gallery of the Dining Hall, presided over by the Headmaster and Director of Music and the youngest chorister. At the Cutlers' Company, the Boar's Head is processed around their Hall by the Master Chef to the accompaniment of the music Caput Apri Defero. At the College it is a splendid sight with all the pupils lining the cloisters to encourage the choir as they pass.

Representing the Company, I attended the 50th Anniversary Service commemorating the Blitz, inaugurated by the London Fire Service and attended by HRH the Princess of Wales. I also planted our Company Cross in the Garden of Remembrance in November, visited the Council for the Care of Churches and had a whole host of other events. It was a full year and had I still been a Headmaster it would have been impossible to arrange my timetable and programme to fit in all these events. I was also involved in negotiations with the Design Museum in London (together with the Masters of the Tallow Chandlers and Lightmongers) to set up a permanent exhibition of the history of lighting. A Buckingham Palace Garden Party, to which Diana and I were invited, and a visit to the Camphill Trust in Botton Village in Yorkshire, which supplies the wax candles for the Company and for the Company's annual presentation for use at the High Altar of St Paul's Cathedral, rounded off the year memorably.

Above all it was a year in which we made many new friendships which have continued, thanks in part to the Association of Past Masters and Prime Wardens 1990-1991 of which I am secretary, and which meets twice a year, one lunch, one dinner, in a variety of the Livery Halls. It was particularly interesting to visit on behalf of the Company, Christ's Hospital, the City of London Freemen's School, King Edward's School Witley and Lord Mayor Treloar College at Alton. They are all foundations which are supported by the City of London and by various Livery Companies. Lord Mayor Treloar is the most remarkable place. Almost all the pupils there are in wheelchairs and some are very physically handicapped yet they achieve great things academically and in a variety of activities, sporting, dramatic and indeed most of the activities found in a school for pupils who are not troubled physically in any way. The staff are a remarkable group of dedicated people and it is a source of great pride to us that our middle daughter, Helen, teaches there and is particularly concerned with communication skills.

When I pause to think about it, it is remarkable to me and a great delight, that two of our daughters have gone into teaching and the third engaged in teaching also but in her case, equestrianism. When I was actively engaged in headmastering, I had often thought that as much as I enjoyed it, it was a 24-hour day, seven day a week commitment in a boarding school. One result I am sure was a neglect of my own family and an immense burden put on my wife. I remember one occasion in Elizabeth's last year at St Swithun's School. She was much involved in sport and music there, representing the school at swimming, tennis and lacrosse, playing the flute in the orchestra and singing in the choir. She asked if I was going down to see her play in a match, adding 'You have never been to see me play'. Sadly this was true for there were always events in my own school, which had necessitated my presence and so Diana had gone down on her own.

Elizabeth had been a bit of a rebel at school and continued this when she got to Cambridge. She had taken A levels in French, German and English, which required a vast amount of reading and then announced that she was going to train as a teacher. She obtained a place at Homerton College and embarked on a period when she appeared at home with varying way-out hairstyles and dress and a strong northern accent, which she knew would annoy me and to which I rose every time. We had a long period of difficult relationships throughout which Diana was the peacemaker, but I am glad to say that now we have the happiest and warmest of times together. Her training was not of the easiest. There was, and still is in many educational training establishments, a very definite prejudice against independent schools and she had to refrain from stating her wish and intention to teach in an independent preparatory school. In her teaching practice she was sent to a fairly tough primary school in Cambridge itself but survived it and found that teaching really did appeal to her. By the end of the four years she had worked her rebelliousness out of her system and to my great delight got a job at Holmewood House School at Langton Green, one of the most prestigious schools in the South of England. Here she soon established herself as an outstandingly good teacher, prepared to give herself fully to her pupils. She also met a colleague, Paul Gripper, to whom she is now happily married. However, things did not work out for her there and she decided to leave. Her next post was at St Aubyns at Rottingdean, a wonderfully traditional boys' boarding prep school run by Julian and Hilary James, the very best type of prep school couples.

While at Cambridge it had been constantly stressed to her and her fellow students that in no circumstances whatsoever should they ever touch a pupil – for fear of legal assault from parents! At the interview she asked Julian whether, if a pupil hurt himself, she was allowed to comfort him or would that mean her leaving her job. The reply was 'You would lose your job if you didn't'! Julian had been a pupil of mine at Charterhouse (though I only told Elizabeth this after she had been offered the job) and I was so glad that she was working for him. She had several very happy years at St Aubyns and then returned to Holmewood House where she became housemistress of the girls' boarding house. By now she had a little girl, Lucy, with another baby on the way. After several very happy and successful years in which Lucy was really growing up in a family with several 'older sisters' and Harry was adored by all, the school decided to close down the girls boarding house and Elizabeth devotes herself to being a full-time mum whilst giving Paul, now a senior master at the school, every support.

Helen our second daughter was a much more conforming pupil at St. Swithun's and ended up, to our great joy, as Head Girl. She was also involved in sport and music. Having started out learning the clarinet, she found that there was an excess of clarinettists and so turned to the bassoon, which she played in the school orchestra. She is one of those fortunate people who can turn their hand to any musical instrument they come across. On leaving school she decided to train as a nurse and went as a student nurse to Westminster Hospital in London. She enjoyed the work but was

The family grows, 1993.

constantly in trouble for 'spending too much time talking and listening to the patients', which has always seemed to me one of the main justifications for being a nurse. She suddenly arrived home and announced that she had resigned. If only she had talked to us we would have suggested a move to a smaller, regional hospital but the die was cast. She then found a job which really appealed as an instructor at an outward bound/ mountaineering centre in North Wales. She has always enjoyed swimming, sailing, rock climbing, canoeing etc. and was in her element there. But after a few months she came back to the South of England to become assistant matron at another very good prep school, Aldro at Shackleford near Godalming (where I had had my first experience as Headmaster-elect with their sports day). After a while she announced to us that she was bringing a colleague home to meet us, Malcolm Cronshaw, now our son-in-law. He teaches Mathematics and sport and is the ideal of the prep school master. They were married in the Chapel at Hurstpierpoint College, by kind permission of the Headmaster, by our old friend Bill Peters, formerly Chaplain of Brighton College and now Vicar of Uckfield. It was good to be back in the Chapel, scene of our own immensely joyful wedding in 1966 and everyone enjoyed the day. We returned to Hanbury Cottage at Cocking after the reception and my mother amazed us all by sitting up with us in the garden until past midnight. Helen was in fact the first daughter to be married and Elizabeth followed two years later though she was married in the village Church (again by Bill Peters) with the reception in a wonderful old Sussex barn nearby.

Helen now has a son, Ben, who is eleven and a daughter, Hannah, who is nine. They are both at school in Petersfield which has splendid state schools at all levels. Ben, to his father's delight, is a very good soccer player and plays for the Petersfield eleven year old team. He is also learning the trombone and both children are doing well at school. Helen is teaching at Lord Mayor Treloar College as I mentioned earlier and Malcolm remains at Aldro.

So, I have two daughters and two sons-in-law engaged in education – something of which I could never have dreamt and which makes me very happy.

Caroline, our youngest daughter, had been riding a pony almost before she could walk. Of the three, she was clearly the one who took the greatest delight in riding. After being a day girl to Handcross Park, a prep school about 15 miles from Hurstpierpoint, where she was reasonably happy, her great wish was to follow her sisters to St Swithuns. She sat the Common Entrance at the appropriate time but after gaining her O levels she wished to go to an equestrian centre to do her training.

She went to West Wolves at Ashington to take her BHS examinations and then went on to Wellington Riding, a centre just south of Reading, to gain her BHS Instructor Diplomas. She had just completed these when I met Lavinia Duchess of Norfolk, who had become a great friend after a number of visits to Hurstpierpoint. She asked after all the family and I gave her the news saying in conclusion that Caroline had just finished at Wellington and now wanted to work in a racing stables. It was not said with any particular intent but the next morning the telephone rang after breakfast. 'Roger, it's Lavinia. Is Caroline at home?' When I said that she was, Lavinia continued 'Bring her down this morning to see my daughter at Angmering Park'. Her daughter was, of course, Lady Anne Herries the racehorse trainer. We drove down and the first person I met was Colin Cowdrey, who was married to Lady Anne. He and I chatted together while Caroline went off to be put through her paces. She came back two hours later grinning from ear to ear. She had acquitted herself well and was offered a job as stable lad, accommodation provided.

As the only girl in the yard she was 'tested' by the lads. On one occasion soon after she started there I met her and on asking how she was, was told, 'My arms are six inches longer!' She had been put on a 17-hand stallion but she had stayed on and proved herself. She led up for various well-known jockeys including Lester Piggott and Frankie Dettori and then was given her apprentice jockey licence by Lady Anne. The first big race she was in was at Kempton Park. I was at a conference in Cambridge and could not be there but I telephoned in for the result and learnt that she had won! A great cause for rejoicing. I learnt later from Caroline what had happened. In the jockey's room she had met Frankie Dettori who on finding that she was riding in a race asked her if she had walked the course. As she had not, he walked it with her and on finding out she was riding a horse he had ridden gave her the following advice: 'Hold him back so that two furlongs from home you are at the back of the field then give him his head. At one furlong there will only be the champion lady jockey ahead of you. She looks over her left shoulder, so come up on her right and with a bit of luck you will win.' Caroline did exactly as he suggested and won by a short head. We were so delighted for her. She was placed in several other races that season.

Caroline was the only unmarried daughter when we received an invitation to a Royal Garden Party at Buckingham Palace in 1991 so we were able to take her with us. We had a splendid day and it was another of the many perks attached to being Master of a City Livery Company.

We had had the good fortune in 1987 of going to the Palace to another Garden Party with all three daughters thanks to the kind offices of our Lord Lieutenant, at that time Lavinia Duchess of Norfolk, whom I had got to know when at Hurstpierpoint and for whose daughter Caroline was working as a stable lad. I was indeed the proud husband and father with four glamorous female companions. As we walked into the gardens one of the Gentlemen at Arms came up to speak to us. He was a former parent and to the girls' great delight he asked them if they would like to meet a member of the Royal Family. All the senior members were there that day and my personal hope was that the girls would choose the Queen Mother whom I had always longed to meet. I thought however that they would probably choose Princess Diana. Without a moment's hesitation all three replied 'The Princess Royal'. When we were presented, she spoke briefly but graciously to Diana and to me and then asked Elizabeth what she was doing. When Elizabeth replied, 'Training to be a teacher,' the response came, 'You must be mad!' Helen's reply of training to be a nurse brought the comment, 'That's a bit better!' but Caroline's response 'I am a stable lad with Lady Herries' had the result that she and the Princess Royal had a long and animated conversation about horses, to Caroline's great delight.

We were particularly fortunate to be invited on altogether three occasions which will always remain in the memory.

Caroline had always wanted to go to Australia to work and this she did, finding a post with the Freedman Brothers in Melbourne. She rode, amongst other horses, the previous year's winner of the Melbourne Cup and half way through her year, at the suggestion of her employers, she moved up to another yard of theirs bringing on younger horses and then on to work for another trainer as her

Off to the Palace – Garden Party, 1991.

assistant. We wondered whether she would return to this country but to our great joy she did and is now happily settled in Herefordshire where she has her own small breaking and schooling yard for young racehorses, together with training some point-to-pointers. Her husband, Steve, farms, and apart from turkeys, grows apples, strawberries and Christmas trees and has just installed an apple juicing plant producing very excellent apple juice. They both work immensely hard and are extremely happy. So there is an up to date view of our family and I have every reason to be very proud of all three daughters.

Chapter 14

WHEN RECENTLY I MET a former HMC colleague and told him that I was writing my memoirs he replied: 'Well you should make quite a bit of money out of that – half the members of HMC will pay you to get a mention and the other half will pay you not to put them in!' Of course, much of the work I was doing as Membership Secretary was of a confidential nature and cannot be recorded here!

I suppose that the most frequent problems I had were when a Head had fallen out with his Governors and where it was necessary to intervene on his behalf. This was occasionally more difficult when my sympathies were with the Governors but I hope that I always did my best for the members. I am glad that the Governing Bodies Association (GBA) has now a series of sessions for Governors to inform them, not only of their responsibilities, but also of the many problems in which a Head will need support and, at times, comfort. There were some classic errors made, however. I remember one Headmaster ringing up for advice. Before his appointment, the Governors asked the staff which was their preferred candidate, which was followed by the selection of a different candidate who was now in touch with me. He had had a row with a senior member of staff who had retaliated with the words: 'Well, Headmaster, you are not very popular. After all, you were not the man we wanted'. The Head was put in an impossible situation by a thoughtless action.

Another case in which I was much helped, as on many occasions, by a SHA Field Officer, was where a continually disruptive pupil had been finally expelled by his Head; the parents had appealed to the Governors who reinstated the pupil without reference to the Head! We had a long interview with the Chairman and finally persuaded him that it was vitally necessary for the future well-being of the school and for the authority of the Headmaster to support him and exclude the boy.

A third case was that of a Headmaster who was in his tenth year of his second Headship. He had a two-day Governors' meeting in the course of which the Governors spent the night lodged with various members of staff. Two of these, who did not see eye to eye with the Headmaster, had told their overnight visitors that his man management skills were non-existent and that the whole Common Room had lost confidence in him. The Governors meeting ended and they left the school after lunch. Unbeknown to the Head, they moved to a nearby hotel and had a further meeting after which the Chairman and Vice-Chairman returned to the school and informed the Head that his contract was terminated as from the end of that academic year. He was given no chance to state his views or to try to repair any situation which might be in effect. I went with a former Chairman of HMC to see the Chairman of Governors and after much discussion stated what I proposed to do if they would not reconsider their decision – I fear that what I said does seem rather like blackmail, though I stressed at the time that it was a mere statement of facts. What I said was 'If the Governors persist in their present course of action I shall firstly write to all the current members of HMC to advise them, and any members of their staff who might be interested, not to apply for the post of Headmaster as the Governing Body does not know how to treat a person in that position. Secondly I shall ask the Secretary of SHA to write to all his members in a similar vein, and thirdly if in spite of that you manage to appoint someone, I shall ensure that he is not elected into membership of HMC'. After a pause, the outcome was that our member was given two years and the opportunity to resign gracefully.

Life was not continually fraught with problems, however. One of the most enjoyable aspects of my job was to attend each of the seven Divisional meetings once a year and I combined this with a visit to three or four schools in that area. I also visited each Head new in post during his first year and this, together with visits that involved some problem and visits to inspect new members, meant that in the course of my eleven years I visited 209 of the 240 member schools (most of those I did not see were in Scotland or Northern Ireland). HMC was, and I trust still is, a very happy 'club' as well as what it has now become – a powerful voice in the world of education. It has had over many years a succession of able, eminent and wise men as Chairmen and the Secretary who took over from me the educational and political aspects, Vivian Anthony, did a magnificent job in promoting HMC's influence and importance nationally.

Another immensely interesting and enjoyable part of being Membership Secretary was that it involved organizing the Annual Meeting each year. For many years this had been held alternately at Oxford and Cambridge in one of the larger Colleges. There was then a move to bring in one of the more modern universities every other year, which meant that we had the chance to visit and meet the staff of a wide variety of institutions. In 1988 we went to the University of Swansea where I had the opportunity to welcome all members and guests in Welsh and where we were most splendidly looked after.

In 1990, we went to the University of Aberdeen, my first visit to that remarkable city. The Chairman was David Jewell, the Master of Haileybury, who provided us with a wonderful array of guest speakers including Malcolm Rifkind and Field Marshal Lord Bramall, with the highlight of a wonderful address from the then Archbishop of Canterbury, Robert Runcie – the only occasion in my thirty-three years in membership of HMC that a visiting speaker was given an immediate and spontaneous standing ovation by all the members. This Annual Meeting stands out in my memory for two other reasons. I had had to go into hospital early that summer for yet another operation on my feet – my toes had begun once again to double over each other causing pain and a general loss of balance. On this occasion there was no nine-month period of both feet in plaster, as had happened when I was sixteen, but by the time of the Annual Meeting I was still on two arm crutches which made manoeuvrability round the vast campus rather difficult – but everyone was most sympathetic and helpful. The other memory is of when David Jewell and I paid a preliminary visit to the University to arrange accommodation etc. The very formidable Scottish housekeeper, Miss Macpherson, had asked me how many rooms we required, to which I replied '290 single rooms and two doubles, one for the Chairman and his wife and one for me and my Secretary'. The atmosphere became decidedly chilly until David, convulsed with laughter said, 'Roger, you had better explain to Miss Macpherson that your Secretary is also your wife!'

It reminded me of an incident at a Schools Council meeting soon after Diana had joined me at HMC. In a crowded room with delegates from all the Unions with teaching connections, there was a telephone call for me from my Secretary. At the end of a short conversation I said, 'Thank you darling that's fine – see you tonight'! I turned to find the whole room staring at me. To my embarrassed statement 'My Secretary is also my wife', Fred Jarvis of the NUT replied, 'What a pity – my opinion of the independent school world was going up!'

The 1992 Annual Meeting was remarkable for three reasons – firstly, we went abroad, secondly wives were invited to participate for the first time and thirdly we were in hotels and not university rooms. The reason for all this was the remarkable 1992 Chairman, Father Dominic Milroy OSB, the Headmaster of Ampleforth. I think that for some years some members had felt that unlike other professional associations we did not invite our spouses to our annual get-togethers. It being 1992, the year of the start of the Common Market, Dominic felt that we should go abroad with wives and so I was despatched by HMC to visit Paris, Amsterdam and Brussels as possible venues. Paris would have been immensely expensive and so would Amsterdam. When I was staying with the Headmaster of the British School of Brussels he suggested that I ought to look at Bruges. We went there together and I was immediately captivated by the place. Also it became clear that whereas to the other capital cities of the three countries we were just another crowd of visitors, in Bruges the City Fathers would warmly welcome us. We were offered the magnificent Belfry, a mediaeval hall, for our meetings, a reception in the City Hall given by the Mayor and immense help in all the arrangements by the Tourist Office.

I reported back favourably to the Committee and was told to go ahead with arrangements. We were to be lodged in three hotels, all within easy walking distance of the Belfry, and I allocated members to these. Unfortunately one of the three was not so satisfactory, which caused me some sharp comments but after our official complaint to their head office, things improved. Our Annual Service was held in the magnificent Bruges Cathedral and Cardinal Basil Hume, a lifelong friend and fellow monk of Dominic Milroy, came over to preach and with him came the trebles from Westminster Cathedral, giving us a most memorable occasion.

The Annual Dinner was equally remarkable – served in the Belfry with staff in mediaeval costume and a perambulating 'oompah' band which in the course of a long evening encouraged many of those present to dance during and after the meal. Geoffrey Parker, the Vice-Chairman and High Master of Manchester Grammar School, arose to make his speech at five minutes to midnight! It was a very amusing and interesting speech and held everyone's attention.

After-dinner speeches have caused some concern at Annual Meetings. One need never worry about the speech from the current Vice-Chairman (the previous year's Chairman of HMC) as one invariably gets a good entertainment. Those who propose the health of the Conference can vary. In the minds of most older members of HMC is the speech we were given at the University of Exeter in the 1970s by the Professor of Mathematics (standing in for the Vice Chancellor) who spoke for some 35 minutes on the history of Mathematics and as he sat down had to be reminded to propose the toast. At the first Annual Meeting I ran in 1986 at the University of Leeds, the gentleman who was to speak asked me what was required. I replied, 'We will have worked hard for two days and everyone will really appreciate a short, humorous address' – I then reassured colleagues that all would be well – and we were given some 22 minutes on the history of Education! Some speeches do remain in the memory for the right reasons, however, most notably an hilarious offering from a Canon at Christ Church, Oxford, which was generally reckoned by older members present to be the best heard for many years.

Since Bruges, we have tended to go to hotels with conference facilities which seems to be the more popular venues for our members, though a few still hanker after the non-sybaritic rigours of some University campuses.

The post of HMC Membership Secretary, or Assistant Secretary of SHA responsible for HMC schools, as it was when I was appointed, had in previous years been held by former Headmasters who had retired at the age of 60 and who took it on for three, four or five years. I had been appointed at age 54 to provide continuity and take it on for a longer spell and so it was at the Annual Meeting in 1996 held in Glasgow that I was given a wonderful farewell by all my colleagues and friends, although I was, in fact, not to retire until Summer 1997. It was felt that the Annual Meeting was the one occasion of the year when virtually all members would be present, and so it turned out. We were staying in two large hotels in the centre of Glasgow but the Annual Dinner was held in the Great Hall of the Kelvingrove Art Museum. Glasgow City Council did us proud and entertained us to a champagne reception in the Museum after it had closed to the general public so that we had the great privilege of being able to wander round and see all that the museum had to offer. We then had a magnificent Scottish feast, entertained by pipers from one of our member schools and I was presented with a set of engraved decanters, each on its own wooden and brass stand. It was certainly quite an ordeal to make a speech to what is surely one of the most critical audiences you could find but they seemed to enjoy what I said and it was for Diana and me a happy and memorable occasion.

It was yet another successful Annual Meeting, the eleventh I had organized and most of them with Diana's help. To our great joy, HMC invited her to continue to organize the Annual Meetings, although there would not be the same involvement in HMC affairs, and this she did for a further three years with conspicuous success, notably dealing with a gathering in Brighton which included a talk from the Princess Royal and an after dinner speech from the King of the Hellenes, both of which necessitated much co-operation with the police and special branch.

There were nine more months to go after Glasgow and before I ceased working for HMC. They passed quickly and on the whole uneventfully. One of the annual events which I greatly enjoyed was the training course which we laid on each April for Heads taking up their new appointments in the following September. A senior HMC member would run it with three other practising Heads, and an input from the Secretaries of the Bursars' Association, the Medical Officers of Schools Association and the Governing Bodies Association to highlight various aspects of headmastering which may dominate the life of a Head. We would also have a Headmaster who had been in post for a year to come and give his views on what it had been like.

In one of his books, John Rae, the former Headmaster of Westminster School, wrote of the qualities needed in a Headmaster: 'A thick skin, a quick wit, stamina, a steady nerve, political dexterity, a capacity for ruthlessness and a keen sense of the absurd'. Whilst all these do seem to me to be a necessary part of each Headmaster's make up, I am more inclined to agree with

Michael Charlesworth, the doyen of Shrewsbury School which he has served throughout his whole life, when he wrote on the desirable headmagisterial qualities: academic distinction; administrative ability; flair for public relations, especially with parents; skill in communication with staff and pupils; judgement – particularly in the choice of staff; vision; and a touch of charisma: leaders must be seen to lead – and he should know, having served under seven Headmasters and been one himself!

I hope that we got some of this across to those 'new boys' who attended our courses. They were certainly rewarding courses to run and a great way to get to know one's future members. My follow up visits to them in their schools were equally enjoyable. What a great variety there is within the establishments that make up the Headmasters' Conference, though I am now out of date to be giving it that title for it is now the Headmasters' and Headmistresses' Conference, though still known by the acronym HMC. This does not mean that we have taken the place of the Girls' Schools Association (GSA) which still flourishes as the Association of Heads of Girls' Independent Schools. When I became a member of HMC in 1964 there were 225 Heads in membership, all of boys only schools. In 1997 there were 242 Heads in membership though less than 60 of these schools were now boys only. Co-education is now firmly established and over half the schools are fully co-educational with the remaining quarter with girl pupils in the Sixth Form – and gradually these too are converting to full co-education. As a result there have been some female Heads appointed and hence the change in the title of the Conference. I believe that there are now ten of these ladies in membership.

While I was at Hurstpierpoint it remained a wholly boys' school. I was not, and am not, opposed to the idea of co-education. I do feel and always have felt, however, that whilst there are many children who thrive in a co-educational atmosphere there are still some, both boys and girls, who will do better in a single sex institution. At Hurst, we had several girls' schools in the area with whom we could join for social and cultural activities but I retained it as a boys' school. A further reason for this was that if parents wished to have a Woodard School education for their children then in Sussex we could offer the full choice – Lancing with girls in the Sixth Form, Ardingly fully co-educational, St. Michael's Burton Park, Petworth girls only and Hurstpierpoint boys only. How things have changed. Since I left in 1986 Lancing, Ardingly and Hurstpierpoint are all fully co-educational and St. Michael's has closed! However, at the time it seemed to me the right thing to do and as then the only all boys boarding school in Kent, Sussex and Hampshire apart from ourselves were Tonbridge and Winchester (academically in a different league from us) and Worth (Roman Catholic) this was a further justification. But times have indeed changed and I have just seen from an advertisement for Hurst in our local paper 'Fully co-educational, 5-day week, day, flexi, weekly and full boarding options'.

The Summer Term 1997 drew to a close. I sorted through mounds of papers, files and books and loaded up the car. We drove to Leicester and deposited everything in the office of my successor David Prince, formerly Headmaster of Reed's School Cobham, and returned to our cottage in Sussex, wondering whether retirement would be a good thing or not.

Chapter 15

So MANY TIMES in my life I have heard people say 'I am so busy in retirement that I don't know how I found the time to do anything when I was working.' Certainly the weeks pass by so quickly that I often wonder that myself.

The first noticeable difference in my existence is that for perhaps the first time in my life I really do read the newspaper. At school and indeed when working for HMC it was a quick glance at it and then on with the business of the day. Now after breakfast I sit down and really go through it from cover to cover – well, almost – the business news and the sport take less time! What a great deal of misery there is in the world. This seems to be brought home to us so much in the press, on the radio and television.

I am enjoying retirement greatly, and I have become much involved in the Cathedral in Chichester. When we first moved to Cocking we went to our lovely little local Church (11th century) but after a lifetime spent in large ecclesiastical buildings with splendid music, I found that a very small congregation and a few hymns taken at funereal speed and pitched far too high for comfort was a disappointment. Admittedly I had been very fortunate – the music at Lancing was of a high quality, then King's College Cambridge, New College, Oxford, Westminster Abbey (for six months), Paris, Charterhouse and finally Hurstpierpoint had all provided splendid music and services attended by large numbers with full participation of all present. After about six months I decided to go down to the Cathedral each Sunday (after an appropriate apology to our local Rector).

The choir at the Cathedral is the smallest Cathedral choir in England but their style of singing is perfectly attuned to the acoustics of the building and I have had very many happy hours there.

I have been trained as a guide and also act as a doorkeeper, welcoming visitors to the Cathedral. This is a most worthwhile occupation and one meets so many interesting and interested people. Each Friday I am part of a team of five who count the money which has been put in the boxes by visitors. In the summer we count the offerings of two days (and it can be as much as £1,500); in the winter it is the offerings of the preceding four days (and that can be as little as £200 but is usually about £400).

Then on the first Sunday of each month I lead a team of eight to steward at the morning services of Matins and Sung Eucharist. This means handing out books and service sheets, showing visitors to their seats, taking the collection, clearing up after the services and being available to help anyone who is unwell during the service. We get about 400 at each Sunday Eucharist. I also steward at any major event in the Cathedral cycle of worship, notably at Easter, Christmas etc. The Christmas Eve Midnight Mass begins at 11.30 p.m., preceded by three-quarters of an hour of readings and music. All seats in the choir and nave are filled by 11.00 p.m., and the side aisles by 11.20 p.m. and there are usually a hundred or so standing inside the West Door so the Church of England does still flourish at main festival times. One of the most appealing features of the Cathedral is the fact that at the end of the Eucharist the Dean and other senior Cathedral clergy are at the West Door to speak to all those who have attended the service – just as though it were a parish Church, which of course it is for the people of the City of Chichester.

Shortly after we moved to Cocking the then Dean, Robert Holtby, invited me to become a Governor of the Prebendal School, which is the choir school to the Cathedral and now eleven years on I am still a Governor which I enjoy greatly. It is a very happy and successful school with an incredible standard of music amongst its pupils – and not just the Choristers – and concerts given by the pupils are always most rewarding. Up until 13 years ago the Governing Body was the Dean and Chapter but now we have a mix of laity and clergy and the meetings are positive and enjoyable.

So I am much involved with Chichester, which is such an attractive city. There is so much going on there, not only in the Festival Theatre, which has a full programme for the year with in particular a summer season of four plays which attract actors and actresses of the highest calibre, concerts, lectures and events throughout the city which attract many visitors.

This part of Sussex really does have much to offer. Each year there are also the Petworth and the Arundel festivals with music and drama, and then of course we have Goodwood racecourse only three miles from our cottage and Fontwell a further eight miles on. The summer sees polo at Cowdray Park in Midhurst, two and a half miles north and then there is the excellent train service from Haslemere to London – four trains every hour, the longest journey being just under the hour. Haslemere is only 11 miles north of Cocking but I find that with so much music and theatre close to hand we do not go as frequently to London as in the past.

I have been a member of the National Trust for over thirty years and am now a room steward at Petworth House for the summer season each year – April to the end of October. Every other Tuesday I arrive at the house at 12.45 p.m. for a briefing on the day's events and then steward from 1.00 p.m. until 5.30 p.m. One of the best features is that one is in a different room each time so that one has the opportunity to get to know the whole of the house open to the public. Each room is equipped with an excellent 'crib' for the steward in case of awkward questions from visitors and of course the house contains the largest and best collection of paintings in the whole National Trust. The artist, Turner, was given a studio in the house by the third Earl of Egremont and produced some splendid works of art of the grounds. There are at least 20 Turners on show together with a number of paintings by Van Dyck and individual works from other masters. The afternoons at Petworth are always instructive and enjoyable.

So where does the rest of my time go? We see the family quite frequently. Helen and Malcolm are only 15 minutes away in Petersfield, Elizabeth and Paul about 90 minutes east at Crowborough and so the grandchildren are often in evidence. Caroline and Steve are further away of course, three and a quarter hours to Leominster but they are immensely welcoming and hospitable and we go up to stay fairly frequently.

For some years now I have driven to South Wales once a month to visit my mother. My parents had lived on in Barry with my father continuing to practise as a solicitor until he retired in 1970. My brother and I tried to persuade him to keep a few longstanding clients but he resolved to retire completely, which was not a good idea. He was no longer playing any bowls and did not have any real hobbies, so that life was rather routinely dull. Neither of my parents had many friends but lived quietly and happily content with their own company. Sadly my father was found to have leukaemia and died in 1979 at the relatively early age of 77.

We felt that my mother would be lost on her own so she came to live with us at Hurstpierpoint but it did not work out for various reasons. She knew nothing of the school world and found it difficult to fit into the pattern of life. She also found it lonely without anyone of her own age. After eighteen months with us she went to live with my brother and his family in Cardiff, but this too proved unsatisfactory. We decided that we must find a residential home for her as she could not possibly live on her own. Fortunately after a couple of poor shots, we found a residential home in Llandaff, near the Cathedral and where she was wonderfully cared for. She had her own room with all her own possessions around her and lived happily there for nearly twenty years, dying just before her 96th birthday in 2000. Up until six months before her death she had continued to complete the main Daily Telegraph crossword each day and she was kept going by the television with an unrivalled

My parents (about 1976).

knowledge of golf, snooker and darts! I feel that she had a good and happy life.

One of the intriguing things about moving into a small village is that it takes a long time to be accepted by the long-standing inhabitants. Now after nearly sixteen years we are accepted. Diana has become very involved with the Church and is the Secretary of the PCC. Our recently arrived Rector is full of ideas and determined to involve the village in community activities, so a Lunch Club for the over 60s, a Toddlers' Group for the young and functions in the Church are all flourishing. These together with the recent changes in the Church of England services and rosters for sidesmen, flower arrangers and church cleaning mean that Diana seems almost as busy as she was when she was working for HMC but she enjoys it and she is as involved with people as when we were at the College.

Last Christmas (2001) for my seventieth birthday I was given two very splendid presents from members of the family. The first was a row of vines for two years at a vineyard just south of Bordeaux, the Chateau Rousselle. Apart from various events organized in England and in France throughout the year for members of 3D Wines, as the organization is known, one can go down in the summer to collect one's own wine – it is reckoned that a row of vines will produce 4 cases of wine per year, so this will add an extra sparkle to my yearly visit to France. There will also be the joy of telling guests to our house that we are about to drink 'our own wine'. The other present was the gift of membership of the Elite Racing Club which gives me a share in the ownership of 20 horses which are in training with various establishments around the country and which will enable us to attend various racecourses for different meetings.

So with wine and horses I have two further and immediate interests for the future.

So here I am now coming to the end of these meandering memoirs. When I was asked a year ago to write them I could not believe that anyone would be interested in what has been a very usual sort of life. I just hope that what I have written has held your attention and amused you. I know that I have indeed been fortunate for I have had a wonderfully happy life (prep school apart). I have been lucky in my work, lucky in my friends, lucky in my family. I have just celebrated my seventieth birthday – which I hope is just another beginning. I have the Cathedral, Petworth House, the Prebendal School, the Village activities – I am now the Treasurer of the PCC, the Cocking Lunch Club, the History Group (producing our Millennium tribute) and the Toddlers' Group – so I have to keep up with financial matters. There are also the additional interests I have just mentioned – the wine and the horses. And I have the family – my wife and the three girls and their husbands, four grandchildren and my nieces and nephew, and they have just provided me with a great niece and great nephew. Perhaps in 10 years or so someone will again write out of the blue to ask me to add to my memoirs. I shall be ready and willing.

Index

Aldro School 133, 185
Anne, Princess Royal 188, 196
Anthony, Vivian 192
Ardingly 27, 134, 198
Arrowsmith, Bob 71
Authers, David 175

Ball, Peter & Michael 19, 22, 36
Bancroft, Donald 33
Barry, Glamorgan 1-9, 39, 202
Bartlett family 87, 90, 152
Beatrice (nanny) 1, 8, 10
Beer, Ian 165
Berry, Winifred 158
Bertrand, Claude 60, 66
Beves, Donald 43-5, 48, 49
Birch, John 160
Birley, Sir Robert 159-60
Boar's Head Feast 181
Bolgar, Dr Robert 44, 48
Boyden, Frank 91-2
Britten, Benjamin 26, 47
Brown, Capt John 112
Bruges 195
Bury, Robert 145, 153
Buss, Gerald 130

Carleton, John 53-4, 65
Chamberlain, Christopher 22-6, 32, 37, 38
Chapman, Shirley 174
Chare, Kenneth 68
Charterhouse 65-82
Chaventré, Robin & Carolyn 179
Chichester Cathedral 199-200
Clark, Roger 45
College Franco-Britannique 60

Dancy, John 46, 57
Day, Tony 72
Dean, Christopher 153
Denning, Lord 160
Dept of Education, Oxford 52, 60, 64
Derry, Rev. Wilfred 30, 37, 57, 71
Dettori, Frankie 187
Doherty, Frank 19-22

Edinburgh, Philip Duke of 72-3, 165
Eggar, John 138
Elizabeth, Queen 72-3
Evans, Dick 125
Evesque, Denis 60, 66
Ewer, Johnny 19

Fisher, Robson 166, 168
Flood, Dick 82, 84
Florey, Frank 147
Forster, E.M. 43, 47, 51
Fuller, A.R.B. (Fats) 76-78

Ganz, Timothy 130
Gardiner, Peter 73
Garten, Dr Hugo 53, 58, 59
Gilbert, Mollie 76
Glyndebourne 47, 155
Green, Mark 131
Griffiths Bill (father) 1-2, 4-7, 16-17, 41, 46-7, 49, 202
Griffiths Evelyn (mother) 2, 5, 7-8, 10, 12, 41, 49, 202-4
Griffiths, Caroline (daughter of author) 157, 186-9, 202
Griffiths, Diana, née Brown (wife of author) 112-15, 116, 126-8, 149, 152, 157, 163-4, 168, 173, 193, 196, 204

Griffiths, Elizabeth (daughter of
    author) 126-7, 157, 183-4, 188, 202
Griffiths, Granny & Grandpa 2-3, 4,
    5, 16
Griffiths, Helen (daughter of author)
    127, 157, 182, 184-6, 202
Griffiths, Richard (brother of author)
    5-8, 35-6, 46-7, 49, 75, 95

Halcrow, Leonard 67, 71, 94
Halsey, Patrick 32-3
Hamilton, Walter 54-6, 65
Hanbury Cottage 168-9
Handford, Basil 21, 29, 33
Harris, Colin 45
Harrison, Eric 70, 81
Hawkins, Horace 160
Headmasters' Conference (HMC)
    165-8, 173-8, 191-9
Healey, Harry 12-15
Heap, Sir Desmond 160
Henson, Nicky 78
Herries, Lady Anne 188
Hooppell, Marjorie 126
Horsfall, Peg 67
Howard, Ronnie 125
Hughes, David 128
Hurstpierpoint 27, 98ff

Ireby, Audrey 36

Jacks, Maurice 58
Jagger, Sam 18, 36
James, Julian & Hilary 184
Jewell, David 193

King's College, Cambridge 32, 37,
    39-40, 42-51
Kirkby, Florence 166, 174
Kleinwort, Mrs Joan 155
Knowling, Arthur 81
König, Marga 87

Lambert, George 162
Lancing 15, 18-42, 46-7

Las Vegas 151-2
Le Grand, Roland 67, 73
Lickey Hills School 12-15
Llandrindod Wells 6, 8-13, 15-16
Lord Mayor Treloar College 182, 186
Lycée Claude Bernard 60-3

Marble, Pete 86, 88, 92
Marcotte, Marcel 86
Marriott, Martin 52
Mason, Kenneth 107, 123, 163
Mathias, Sir Richard 125
Mauriange family 34
McAdam, Michael 123, 130, 132
Meyrick, Harry 32, 34
Milroy, Fr Dominic 193-4
Moffat Howitt, Rev. 30
Morrell, Lloyd 131
Moylan, Denis 56

Nears, Colin 45
Neville-Smith, Esther 47
New York 84, 89, 149, 152
Norfolk, Lavinia, duchess of 187,
    188
Noyce, Wilfred 68

Ord, Boris 48
Oswald, Philip 45

Paris 35, 60-4
Parnell-Smith, Major 29
Pears, Peter 26, 47
Peters, Bill 186
Petworth House 202
Pomfret School, Connecticut 85-92,
    150
Puttock, Marvin 29

Radcliffe, Philip 48
Redgrave, Corin 59
Rooper, Jasper 26
Rowan-Robinson, Anthony 68
Ruddock, Reg 170
Runcie, Robert 192

Russell Wells, Dr Barbara 26
Saenger, Dr Ernst 32, 53
St Baruc's School 9
Salzburg Festival 73
Searls, Nicholas 130
Sellar, W.E. 78
Sheppard, Sir John 37-8, 51, 52
Smith, Alec 58-9
Smith, Mr & Mrs 42-3
Snape, Peter 166, 174
Stringer, Russell 87, 88, 91

Temperley, Nicholas 45
Thomas, Dick 100, 125
Thorn, John 165
Thorold, Rev. Henry 30-1, 71
Tibbenham, Mrs 8, 12, 15

Timms, Wilfred 68
Trevelyan, Humphrey 45
Twichell, Dave 88, 89

Wallace, Ian 126
Wax Chandlers, Worshipful Company
of 76, 78, 179-81
Waycott, Joe 74
Westminster School 53-8
Widor, C.M. 160
Wightwick, Christopher 32, 34
Wilkinson, Patrick 32, 38
Woodard, Alfred 58, 135
Woodard, Florence 57-8
Woodard, Nathaniel 27-8

Young, Brian 65, 68, 70, 77

Bibliography

Lancing College Magazine
King's College Cambridge   Memoir of Provost Sheppard
                              Memoir of Donald Beves
Walter Hamilton: A Portrait (ed. Donald Wright)
Hurstpierpoint College: The School under the Downs by Peter King